PHILIP YANCEY
FINDING
GOD *in*
Unexpected
PLACES

Moorings
Nashville, Tennessee
A Division of the Ballantine Publishing Group, Random House, Inc.

Thanks to my editor, Tim Jones,
who guided my words through several incarnations.

Contents

Part Four: Finding God Among the Headlines

Part Five: Finding God in the Cracks

Part Six: Finding God Within the Church

Introduction

For several years my wife and I have attended Renaissance Weekends on Hilton Head Island, events that bring together many of the cultural leaders of the United States. At mealtime you may find yourself seated next to an astronaut who walked on the moon, or a Metropolitan Opera singer, or a White House television correspondent. Or maybe even a member of the First Family—the Clintons have attended Renaissance Weekends for more than a decade.

Janet and I have served on panels with admirals, ambassadors, members of Congress, and federal judges. Usually we are introduced as "evangelical Christians," a label that in the Washington Beltway crowd can conjure up strange images indeed. For most of the people at Renaissance Weekend, "evangelical Christian" means the same thing as "Religious Right." They think of fanatics who kill abortion doctors and call for the execution of homosexuals. They think of protestors at political rallies who wave large placards and scream.

The 1990s have seen a marked polarization in U.S. society. As court decisions and the general drift of culture push religion to the fringe, some Christians act more and more as if they belong to a fringe religion. Christians under duress often show a tendency to withdraw from the world, pull up the drawbridge, and retreat behind a protective moat. I feel sad about this trend, because it directly contradicts Jesus' command to act like salt in meat and light in the midst of darkness.

The "castle" into which Christians retreat is the church. That makes me sad as well, because God does not limit himself to the four walls of a sanctuary. Jesus himself looked for God not among the pious at the synagogue, but in a widow who had two pennies left to her name and in a tax collector who knew no formal prayers; he found his spiritual lessons in sparrows sold at a market, and in wheat fields and wedding banquets, and, yes, even in the observations of a half-breed foreigner with five failed marriages. Jesus was a master at finding God in unexpected places.

In my own pilgrimage, I have often looked beyond church walls to find God. Because I grew up in southern fundamentalism, my search for God was blocked by racism and fear and judgment. I heard about grace, but mostly experienced law. In the beautiful, orderly world of nature I first saw glimpses of a Creator who has lavished on us a good and grace-full world. Later, reading the works of Augustine, C. S. Lewis, and Martin Luther King, Jr., convinced me that somewhere Christians lived who knew love as well as judgment. As I began to believe, I found rumors of transcendence—the footprints of God—in many places I had never before thought of looking.

John S. Dunne tells of early Spanish sailors who reached the continent of South America after an arduous voyage. The caravel sailed into the headwaters of the Amazon, an expanse of water so wide the sailors presumed it to be a continuation of the Atlantic Ocean. It never occurred to them to drink the water, since they expected it to be saline, and as a result some of these sailors died of thirst. That scene of men dying of thirst even as their ships floated on the world's largest source of fresh water has become for me a metaphor for our age. Some people starve to death spiritually while all around them manna rots.

Friends tell me that science has pushed God from the scene, even though the DNA explorers who look through microscopes and the cosmologists who look through telescopes increasingly report back awesome wonders for which they have no explanation.

People shake their heads in despair over the state of the world despite the fact that in the last decade six hundred million people gained freedom from the greatest tyranny of our century, with hardly a shot being fired. In Eastern Europe a god fell to earth like an idol knocked from its pedestal by a bolt of lightning, and at its base stood Christians armed with nothing but the power of prayer. In South Africa, the leader of the last theologically racist party on earth led the way toward reconciliation. Why the change? F. W. de Klerk himself gave the reason: after his inauguration, in tears, he told his church that he had felt a calling from God to save all the people of South Africa, even though he knew he would be rejected by his own people.

The job of a journalist is, simply, to see. We are professional eyes. As a Christian journalist, I have learned to look for traces of God. I have found those traces in unexpected places: among the chief propagandists of a for-

> All I ask is that you keep an open mind as you look at the world through my eyes.

merly atheistic nation, in a leprosarium in India and an Atlanta slum and even a Chicago health club, at a meeting of Amnesty International, on the Phil Donahue show, at a weekend retreat with twenty Jews and Muslims, in the prisons of Peru and Chile, and even in the plays of Shakespeare. This book, much of it adapted from my articles for *Christianity Today* and other magazines, is my report of what I have seen in the last few years.

I do not ask you to believe all that I believe, or to walk the same path I have walked. All I ask is that you keep an open mind as you look at the world through my eyes.

PART ONE

Finding GOD Without Really Looking

CHAPTER 1

Rumors of Another World

According to Greek mythology, people once knew in advance their exact day of death. Everyone on earth lived with a deep sense of melancholy, for mortality hung like a sword suspended above them. All that changed when Prometheus introduced the gift of fire. Now humans could reach beyond themselves to control their destinies; they could strive to be like the gods. Caught up in excitement over these new possibilities, people soon lost the knowledge of their death day.

3

Have we moderns lost even more? Have we lost, in fact, the sense that we will die at all?

Although some authors argue as much (such as social theorist Ernest Becker in *The Denial of Death*), I have found that behind the noise of daily life rumors of another world can still be heard. The whispers of death persist, and I have heard them, I believe, in three unlikely places: a health club, a political action group, and a hospital therapy group. I have even detected the overtones—but only overtones—of theology in these unexpected places.

I joined the Chicago Health Club after a foot injury forced me to find alternatives to running. It took a while to adjust to the artificiality of the place. Patrons lined up to use high-tech rowing machines, complete with video screen and an animation pace boat, though Lake Michigan, a real lake requiring real oars, lay empty just four blocks away. In another room, Stairmaster™ machines duplicated the act of climbing stairs—this in a dense patch of high-rise buildings. And I marveled at the technology that adds computer-programmed excitement to the everyday feat of bicycling.

I marveled, too, at the human bodies using all these machines: the gorgeous women wearing black-and-hot-pink leotards, and the huge hunks of masculinity who clustered around the weight machines. Mirrored glass, appropriately, sheathed the walls, and a quick glance revealed dozens of eyes checking out the results of all the sweating and grunting, on themselves and on their neighbors.

The health club is a modern temple, complete with initiation rites and elaborate rituals, its objects of worship on constant and glorious display. I detected a trace of theology there, for such devotion to the human form gives evidence of the genius of a Creator who designed with aesthetic flair. The human person is worth preserving. And yet, in the end, the health club stands as a pagan temple. Its members strive to preserve only one part of the person: the body, the least enduring part of all.

Ernest Becker wrote his book, and died, before the exercise craze gripped America, but I imagine he would see in health clubs a blatant symptom of death-denial. Health clubs, along with cosmetic surgery, baldness retardants, skin creams, and an endless proliferation of magazines on sports, swimsuits, and dieting, help direct our attention away from death toward life. Life in this body. And if we all strive together to preserve our bodies, then perhaps science will one day achieve the unthinkable: perhaps it will conquer mortality and permit us to live forever, like Gulliver's toothless, hairless, memoryless race of Struldbrugs.

Once, as I was pedaling nowhere on a computerized bicycle, I thought of philosopher Søren Kierkegaard's comment that the knowledge of one's own death is the essential fact that distinguishes us from animals. I looked around the exercise room wondering just how distinguished from the animals we modern humans are. The frenzied activity I was participating in at that moment—was it merely one more way of denying or postponing death? As a nation, do we grow sleek and healthy so that we do not have to think about the day our muscular bodies will be not pumping iron, but lying stiff in a casket?

Sixteenth-century church reformer Martin Luther told his followers, "Even in the best of health we should have death always before our eyes [so that] we will not expect to remain on this earth forever, but will have one foot in the air, so to speak." His words seem quaint indeed today when most of us, pagan and Christian alike, spend our days thinking about everything but death. Even the church focuses mainly on the good that faith can offer *now:* physical health, inner peace, financial security, a stable marriage.

> The health club is a modern temple, its objects of worship on constant and glorious display.

Physical training is of some value, the apostle Paul advised his protégé Timothy, but godliness has value for all things, holding promise for both the present life and the life to come. As I pedaled, straining against computer-generated hills, I had to ask myself: What is my spiritual counterpart to the Chicago Health Club? And then, more troubling: How much time and energy do I devote to each?

For two years I attended monthly meetings of a local chapter of Amnesty International. There I met good people, serious people: students and executives and professionals who gather together because they find it intolerable blithely to go on with life while other people are being tortured and killed.

Amnesty International's local chapters use an absurdly simple technique to combat human rights abuses: they write letters. Our group adopted three prisoners of conscience: Jorge, a union leader for employees of the Coca Cola Company in Chile, and Ahmad of Pakistan and Joseph of Poland, both of whom were serving long-term sentences for "unpatriotic activity." Each week we would discuss their fates and report on the letters we had written to esteemed officials in their respective countries.

As we sat in a comfortable townhouse eating brownies and fresh vegetables and sipping coffee, we tried to envision how Jorge and Ahmad and Joseph were spending their days and evenings. Letters from their families gave us agonizing insight into their hardships. Despite our efforts to resist it, most of the time a vague feeling of powerlessness pervaded the room. We had received no word from Jorge in two years, and Chilean officials no longer answered our letters. Most likely, he had joined "the disappeared."

The tone of earnest concern in the group reminded me of many prayer meetings I had attended. Those, too, focused group energy on specific human needs. Yet at Amnesty International no one dared pray, a fact that perhaps added to the sense of helplessness. Although the organization was founded on Christian principles, any trace of sectarianism had long since disappeared.

Here is a strange thing, I thought one evening. A worthy organization exists for the sole purpose of keeping people alive. Thousands of bright, dedicated people congregate in small groups centered on that singular goal. But one question is never addressed: Why should we keep people alive?

I have asked that question of Amnesty International staff members, provoking a response of quiet horror. The very phrasing of the question seemed heretical to them. *Why* keep people alive? The answer is self-evident, is it not? Life is good; death is bad (I presume they meant animal life is good, since we were munching vegetable life as we spoke).

These staff members missed the irony that Amnesty International came into existence because not all people in history see their equation as self-evident. To Hitler, to Stalin, to Saddam Hussein, death can be a good if it helps accomplish other goals. No ultimate value attaches to any one human life.

Amnesty International recognizes the inherent worth of every human being. Unlike, say, the Chicago Health Club, AI does not elevate beautiful specimens of perfect health: the objects of our attention were mostly bruised and beaten, with missing teeth and unkempt hair and signs of malnutrition. But what makes such people worthy of our care? To put it bluntly, Is it possible to honor the image of God in a human being if there is no God?

To raise such questions at an Amnesty International meeting is to invite a time of stern and awkward silence. Explanations may follow. *This is not a religious organization. . . . We cannot deal with such sectarian views. . . . People have differing opinions. . . . The important issue is the fate of our prisoners. . . .*

In our strange society, it seems the questions most worth asking are the questions most ignored. The French mathematician Blaise Pascal lived during the early Enlightenment era when Western thinkers first began scorning belief in a soul and the afterlife, matters of doctrine that seemed to them primitive and unsophisticated. Pascal said of such people, "Do they profess to have delighted us by telling us that they hold our soul to be only a little wind and smoke, especially by telling us this in a haughty and self-satisfied tone of voice? Is this a thing to say gaily? Is it not, on the contrary, a thing to say sadly, as the saddest thing in the world?"

I still belong to Amnesty International and contribute money to it. I believe in their cause, but I believe in it for different reasons. Why do strangers such as Ahmad and Joseph and Jorge deserve my time and energy? I can think of only one reason: They bear the sign of ultimate worth, the image of God.

Amnesty International teaches a more advanced theology than the Chicago Health Club, to be sure. It points past the surface of skin and shape to the inner person. But the organization stops short—for what makes the inner person worth preserving, unless it be a soul? And for that very reason, shouldn't Christians lead the way in such issues as human rights? According to the Bible all humans, including Jorge and Ahmad and Joseph, are immortal beings who still bear some mark of the Creator.

Members of the Chicago Health Club do their best to defy or at least forestall death. Amnesty International works diligently to prevent it. But another group I attended faces death head-on, once a month.

I was first invited to Make Today Count, a support group for people with life-threatening illnesses, by my neighbor Jim, who had just been diagnosed with terminal cancer. There we met other people, mostly in their thirties, who were battling such diseases as multiple sclerosis, hepatitis, muscular dystrophy, and cancer. For each member of the group, all of life had boiled down to two issues: surviving and, failing that, preparing for death.

We sat in a hospital waiting area on molded plastic chairs of a garish orange hue (doubtless chosen to make the institution appear more cheerful). We tried to ignore the loudspeaker periodically crackling out an announcement or paging a doctor. The meeting began with each member "checking in." Jim whispered to me this was the most depressing part of the meeting, because very often someone had died in the month since the last meeting. The social worker provided details of the missing member's last days and the funeral.

The members of Make Today Count confronted death because they had no choice. I had expected a mood of great somberness, but found just the opposite. Tears flowed freely, of course, but these people spoke easily and comfortably about disease and death. Clearly, the group was the one place they could talk openly about such issues.

Nancy showed off a new wig, purchased to cover the baldness caused by chemotherapy treatments. She joked that she had always wanted straight hair, and now her brain tumor had finally given her an excuse. Steve, a young man with Hodgkin's disease, admitted he was terrified of what lay ahead. His fiancée refused to discuss the future with him at all. How could he break through to her?

Martha talked about death. The disease ALS (Lou Gehrig's disease) had already rendered her legs and arms useless. Now she breathed with great difficulty, and whenever she fell asleep at night there was a danger of death from oxygen deprivation. Martha was twenty-five years old. "What is it you fear about death?" someone asked. Martha thought a minute and then said this: "I regret all that I'm going to miss—next year's big movies, for example, and the election results. And I fear that I will one day be forgotten. That I'll just disappear, and no one will even miss me."

More than any other people I have met, members of the Make To-day Count group concentrated on ultimate issues. They, unlike the Chicago Health Clubbers, could not deny death; their bodies bore *memento mori*, reminders of inevitable, premature death. Every day they were, in Saint Augustine's phrase, "deafened by the clanking chains of mortality." I wanted to use them as examples for my hedonistic friends, to walk down the street and interrupt parties to announce, "We're all going to die. I have proof. Just around the corner is a place where you can see it for yourself. Have you thought about death?"

Yet would such awareness change anyone for more than a few minutes? As one of novelist Saul Bellow's characters put it, the living speed like birds over the surface of water, and one will dive or plunge but not come up again and never be seen again. But life goes on. Five thousand people die in America each day.

One night Donna, a member of the Make Today Count group, told about watching a television program on the public service station. In the program, Elisabeth Kübler-Ross discussed a boy in Switzerland who was dying of an inoperable brain tumor. Kübler-Ross asked him to draw a picture of how he felt. He drew a large, ugly military tank, and behind the tank he drew a small house with trees, grass, sunshine, and an open window. In front of the tank, just at the end of the gun barrel, he drew a tiny figure with a red stop sign in his hand. Himself.

Rumors of Another World

Donna said that picture captured her feelings precisely. Kübler-Ross had gone on to describe the five stages of grief, culminating in the stage of acceptance. And Donna knew she was supposed to work toward acceptance. But she could never get past the stage of fear. Like the little boy in front of the tank, she saw death as an enemy.

Someone brought up religious faith and belief in an afterlife, but the comment evoked the same response in Make Today Count as it had in Amnesty International: a long silence, a cleared throat, a few rolled eyes. The rest of the evening, the group focused on how Donna could overcome her fears and grow toward the acceptance stage of grief.

I left that meeting with a heavy heart. Our materialistic, undogmatic culture was asking its members to defy their deepest feelings. Donna and the small Swiss boy with the brain tumor had, by sheer primal instinct, struck upon a cornerstone of Christian theology. Death is an enemy, a grievous enemy, the last enemy to be destroyed. How could members of a group that each month saw families fall apart and bodies deteriorate before their eyes still wish for a spirit of bland acceptance? I could think of only one appropriate response to Donna's impending death: *Curse you, death!*

There was another aspect of Christian theology too, the one, most sadly, that Make Today Count would not discuss. The Swiss boy had included his vision of heaven in the background, represented by the grass and trees and the cottage with an open window. Any feeling like "acceptance" would only be appropriate if he truly was going somewhere, somewhere like home. That is why I consider the doctrine of heaven one of the most neglected doctrines of our time.

"I think it is very hard for secular men to die," said Ernest Becker, as he turned to God in the last months of his life.

In the Prado museum in Madrid, Spain, there hangs a painting by Hans Baldung (d. 1545) titled *The Stages of Life, with Death.* It seems a deliberate parody of the classical image of "The Three Graces." On the ground lies a newborn child, resting peacefully. Three pale, elongated figures stand over the child. On the left is a nearly nude woman, the archetype of classical beauty, her skin like alabaster, her figure round and smooth, her hair braided into long strands that cascade down her back. To her right stands an old hag with shriveled, sagging breasts and a sharp, angular face. The hag has her right hand on the beautiful woman's shoulder and, with a mocking, toothless sneer, is pulling the young woman toward her.

The hag's left arm is interlocked with that of a third person, a horrid figure straight out of Hieronymus Bosch, the medieval painter with a passion for the grotesque. Man or woman, you cannot tell. Human features have melted down in a macabre, rotting corpse, with long, slender worms crawling out of its cadaver belly. The head is hairless, and nearly a skull. The corpse holds an hourglass.

Hans Baldung's painting restores, visually, what humanity lost after Prometheus. The beautiful woman has regained the knowledge of the hour of death. Birth, youth, old age—we live out each stage under death's shadow.

The painting lacks one image, a vision of a resurrected body. It is hard for us to live in awareness of death; it may be even harder to live in awareness of afterlife. We hope for re-created bodies while inhabiting aged and ailing ones. Charles Williams once admitted that the notion of immortality never seemed to stir his imagination, no matter how hard he tried. "Our experience on earth makes it difficult for us to apprehend a good without a catch in it somewhere," he said.

The apostle Paul wrote these words to people who, like us, could not quite imagine a good without a catch in it somewhere:

> Though outwardly we are wasting away *[despite all attempts at the Chicago Health Club to reverse entropy]*, yet inwardly we are being renewed day by day. For our light and momentary troubles *[Light and momentary! Paul's jailings, beatings, and ship-*

wrecks remind me of the stories of tortured prisoners I hear about at Amnesty International] are achieving for us an eternal glory that far outweighs them all. So we fix our eyes not on what is seen, but on what is unseen. For what is seen is temporary, but what is unseen is eternal. . . .

For while we are in this tent, we groan *[drawn, haggard, chemotherapied faces from the Make Today Count group come to mind]*, and are burdened, because we do not wish to be unclothed but to be clothed with our heavenly dwelling, so that what is mortal may be swallowed up by life. Now it is God who has made us for this very purpose and has given us the Spirit as a deposit, guaranteeing what is to come.

We need a renewed awareness of death, yes. But we need far more. We need a faith, in the midst of our groaning, that death is not the last word, but the next to last. What is mortal will be swallowed up by life. One day all whispers of death will fall silent.

CHAPTER 2

Not Naked Enough

Whenever I moved into the city of Chicago from the suburbs, I was surprised to find the urban atmosphere more sexually charged. Downtown health clubs, billboards, magazine racks, porno shops, and street wear all revealed, well, *more*. Much more.

It seems curious that a culture advancing in sophistication and technology should heighten the emphasis on sexuality, the primal drive that humans share with all animals, but in my travels I have noticed this consistent pattern. In the Amazon jungle, sex has its place, surely, but it ranks somewhere below a successful hunt or a communal feast. In New York or Paris or Tokyo, sex is sine qua non, the Prime Mover that advertisers rely on in order to sell fine wine, computers, and dental floss.

Whenever a Christian writer turns to the subject of sex, I realize, certain defenses go up. Readers expect a moralistic screed against the sex excess in modern society. I, for one, see little value in such an approach. In the first place, moralizing doesn't stand much chance against the raw power of human sexual drives.

More important, I wonder whether the church has used the wrong approach toward sex entirely. Too often the church has treated sexuality as a grave threat, a rival to spirituality. If you're oversexed, why, repress your sexuality and sublimate that energy into a longing for God.

Between the third and tenth centuries, church authorities issued edicts forbidding sex on Saturdays, Wednesdays, and Fridays, and also during the forty-day fast periods before Easter, Christmas, and Whitsuntide, all for religious reasons. They kept adding feast days and days of the apostles to the proscription, as well as the days of female impurity, until it reached the point that, as historian John Boswell has estimated, only forty-four days a year remained available for marital sex. Human nature being what it is, the church's proscriptions were enthusiastically ignored.

I question the motive behind such edicts. Can we so neatly substitute one drive (toward spiritual union) for another (toward physical union)? I doubt it. After all, in the Garden of Eden, when prelapsarian Adam had perfect spiritual communion with God, even then he felt a loneliness and longing that met no relief until God created Eve.

Rather than positioning sexuality and spirituality against each other as rivals, I see them as deeply related. The more I observe our society's obsession with sexuality, the more I sense in it a thirst for transcendence.

My neighbors, in their condominiums, high-rises, and even suburbs have little transcendence left in their lives. Few of them attend church; they believe science has figured out most of the numinous mysteries of the universe, like disease and weather. Except for the New Agers among them, they tend to scoff at superstitious practices like astrology.

But sex—ah, there's a mystery to which normal principles of reductionism do not apply. Sex is not something you can "figure out." Knowing about sex, even taking a degree in gynecology, doesn't diminish its magical power. Probably the closest thing to a supernatural experience my male neighbors ever have is when they watch Michelle Pfeiffer in a clingy red dress, or when they pore over each microdot of the annual *Sports Illustrated* swimsuit issue. Is it any wonder these swimsuit models are often called "goddesses"?

In this view, sex is not a rival to spirituality, but rather a pointer to it. When a society so completely blocks the human thirst for transcendence, should we be surprised that such longings reroute themselves into an expression of mere physicality? Maybe the problem is not that people are getting naked, but that they aren't getting naked enough: we stop at the skin instead of going deeper, into the soul.

I once talked with priest and author Henri Nouwen just after he had returned from San Francisco. He had visited various ministries to people with AIDS, and was moved with compassion by sad stories of sexual promiscuity. "They want love so bad, it's literally killing them," he said.

More and more, I see sex excess as a modern mutation of classical idolatry, a commitment of spirit to something that cannot bear its weight. When God rebuked the Israelites for their idolatry, he was not condemning their urge to worship. Nor did he disapprove of the more immediate urges that pushed them toward idols: a desire for fertility, for good weather, for military success. Rather, he condemned them for seeking those things from senseless hunks of wood and iron instead of from himself.

> The Bible has another word for what enlightened Westerners call addictions.

What the Old Testament calls idolatry, enlightened Westerners call addictions. These, too, are often good things—sex, food, work, chocolate—that outgrow their rightful place and begin to control a person's life. To a member of AA, alcohol represents an "idol" in which he or she invests all hopes and dreams. The idol of alcohol, like the golden calf, cannot bear such total commitment. It always lets you down.

Tellingly, even our secularized society has found but one effective way to break the pattern of addiction: twelve-step programs, all of which require submission to a "Higher Power." In their own desperate ways, these strugglers are searching for an elixir that will quench their thirst for transcendence.

The French priest Jean Sulivan made this observation about modern society: "Human beings are not looking for just anything but for the absolute, even when they believe they are turning away from it, or when they unknowingly repress it in a search for material things." Repression of spirituality is every bit as dangerous as repression of sexuality.

I was thinking some of these thoughts as I read again the account of Jesus' conversation with a Samaritan woman who had been through five husbands and was living with yet another man. Two things struck me. First, I was reminded of Jesus' exquisite tenderness in dealing with people who had failed on some level. In those days the husband initiated divorce: this Samaritan woman had been unceremoniously dumped by five different men.

I was also struck by Jesus' skill in connecting thirst—physical, parched-throat thirst and also the thirst for intimacy—with a thirst for transcendence that only he could resolve. "Everyone who drinks this water will be thirsty again, but whoever drinks the water I give him will never thirst," he said.

This Samaritan "outcast" woman was the first person to whom Jesus openly revealed himself as the Messiah. After the conversation beside a well, this same woman led a wholesale revival in her town. When her deepest thirst was quenched, a thirst she had never even recognized before Jesus named it, all other thirsts took their rightful place.

CHAPTER 3

The Lost Sex Survey

While much of the media was buzzing about a new survey on sex in America released in 1994, I was thinking about a book, *Sex and Culture*, published in 1934. I discovered it in the windowless warrens of a large university library, and I felt like an archaeologist must feel unearthing an artifact from the catacombs.

Seeking to test the Freudian notion that civilization is a by-product of repressed sexuality, the scholar J. D. Unwin studied eighty-six different societies. His findings startled many scholars, above all Unwin himself, because all eighty-six demonstrated a direct tie between absolute monogamy and the "expansive energy" of civilization. In other words, sexual fidelity was the single most important predictor of a society's ascendancy.

Unwin had no religious convictions and applied no moral judgment: "I offer no opinion about rightness or wrongness." Nevertheless, he had to conclude, "In human records there is no instance of a society retaining its energy after a complete new generation has inherited a tradition which does not insist on pre-nuptial and post-nuptial continence."

For Roman, Greek, Sumerian, Moorish, Babylonian, and Anglo-Saxon civilizations, Unwin had several hundred years of history to draw on. He found with no exceptions that these societies flourished, culturally and geographically, during eras that valued sexual fidelity. Inevitably, sexual mores would loosen and the societies would subsequently decline, only to rise again when they returned to more rigid sexual standards.

Unwin seemed at a loss to explain the pattern. "If you ask me why this is so, I reply that I do not know. No scientist does. . . . You can describe the process and observe it, but you cannot explain it." Yet the trend so impressed him that he proposed a special class of "Alpha" citizens in Great Britain. These individuals of unusual promise would take vows of chastity before marriage and observe strict monogamy after marriage, all for the sake of the empire that needed their talents.

Unwin died before fully developing his theory on "the sexual foundations of a new society," but the incomplete results were published in another book, *Hopousia*, with an introduction by Aldous Huxley.

A decade before Unwin did his research, followers of Vladimir Lenin were espousing a very different "Glass of Water" theory about sex. Sexual desire is no more mysterious or sacrosanct than desire for food or water, they declared, and they rewrote the Soviet law book accordingly. That theory soon collapsed and Soviet society became—on the surface at least—almost puritanical about sexual morality.

Today we hear new versions of the Glass of Water theory. "Sex can finally, after all these centuries, be separated from the all-too-serious business of reproduction," proclaimed Barbara Ehrenreich in a *Time* essay. She got specific: "What could be more moral than teaching that homosexuality is a viable life-style? Or that masturbation is harmless and normal? Or that petting, under most circumstances, makes far more sense than begetting? The only ethic that can work in an overcrowded world is one that insists that women are free, children are loved, and sex—preferably among affectionate and consenting adults—belongs squarely in the realm of play."

Ehrenreich's call for the "de-moralization" of sex has about it the incense smell of the 1960s, birth era of the modern sexual revolution. AIDS may have temporarily dampened enthusiasm for unrestrained lovemaking, but I hear few social commentators articulating a coherent sexual ethic. In our reductionistic society, sex is viewed as a purely biological act, like drinking and eating. Once we perfect the technology of protection, we can go back to coupling.

Strangely, though, sex resists reductionism. Jealousy still rears its ugly head and cuckolds still murder their lovers' lovers, as if sexuality involved the joining of lives and not merely genitals. And in an age of unprecedented birth-control options and widespread sex education, our society produces more unwanted pregnancies than ever before.

Frankly, I do not know what to make of J. D. Unwin's theories about sex and culture. His books rest in the catacombs of libraries because he preached a message that few want to hear, and his moral basis for fidelity ("Zip up for the empire!") easily gets overwhelmed by sheer hormonal force. Moreover, his criterion of "expansive energy" looks different in this time of downsizing and anti-imperialism.

> Journalist G. K. Chesterton used to say that a man who knocks on the door of a brothel is knocking for God.

Without realizing it, though, Unwin may have subtly edged toward a Christian view of sexuality, from which modern society has badly strayed. For the Christian, sex is not an end in itself, but rather a gift from God. Like all such gifts, it must be stewarded according to God's rules, not ours.

If we make a god of progress and destroy the planet God gave us to steward, we will destroy ourselves as well. If we worship power and success and construct the greatest civilization the world has ever seen—it, too, will fall, as Unwin's Babelic survey of history surely shows. And if we make a god of sexuality, that god will also fail, in ways that affect the whole person and perhaps the whole society.

Journalist G. K. Chesterton used to say that a man who knocks on the door of a brothel is knocking for God. That statement has always reminded me of Jesus' conversation with the Samaritan woman at the well, in which he used her thirst for love to introduce her to Living Water.

We have two conflicting ways to look at sex, and each involves a paradox. The reductionistic Glass of Water theory unexpectedly elevates sexuality to a place it does not deserve and cannot sustain; as we give it worship, society disintegrates. On the other hand, the Living Water theory ennobles what at first it seems to dethrone, by restoring sex to its rightful place, as a gift of transcendental value.

CHAPTER 4

Looking Up

I have been thinking about the universe lately. The whole thing. After reading some of astronomer Chet Raymo's elegiac prose *(Starry Nights, The Soul of the Night)*, I have been craning my neck upward at odd angles when I encounter a pool of darkness. Living in Chicago, though, I mostly saw the moon, Venus, and the jets' flight path into O'Hare Field, and must take Raymo's word for what lies beyond.

Learning about the universe does little for earthly self-esteem. Our sun, powerful enough to turn white skin bronze and to coax oxygen from every plant on earth, ranks fairly low by galactic standards. If the giant star Antares were positioned where our sun is—93 million miles away—the earth would be inside it! And our sun and Antares represent just 2 of 500 billion stars that swim around in the vast, forlorn space of the Milky Way. A dime held out at arm's length would block 15 million stars from view, if our eyes could see with that power.

From our hemisphere, only one other galaxy, Andromeda, is large enough and close enough (a mere 2 million light-years away) to see with the naked eye. It showed up on star charts long before the invention of the telescope, and until recently no one could know that the little blob of light marked the presence of another galaxy, one twice the size of the Milky Way and home to half a trillion stars. Or that these next-door neighbors were but 2 of 100 billion galaxies likewise swarming with stars.

One reason the night sky stays dark despite the presence of so many luminous bodies is that all the galaxies are hurtling away from each other with astonishing speed. Tomorrow, some galaxies will be 30 million miles

21

farther away from us. In the time it takes to type this sentence, they'll have receded another 5,100 miles.

I saw the Milky Way in full glory once, while visiting a refugee camp in Somalia, just below the equator. Our galaxy stretched across the canopy of darkness like a highway paved with diamond dust. Since that night, when I lay with warm sand at my back far from the nearest streetlight, the sky has never seemed as empty and the earth never as large.

I had spent all day interviewing relief workers about the megadisaster of the moment. Kurdistan, Rwanda, Sudan, Ethiopia—place names change, but the spectacle of suffering has a dreary sameness: mothers with shriveled, milkless breasts, babies crying and dying, fathers foraging for firewood in a treeless terrain.

After three days of hearing tales of human misery, I could not lift my sights beyond that refugee camp situated in an obscure corner of an obscure country on the Horn of Africa. Until I saw the Milky Way. It abruptly reminded me that the present moment did not comprise all of life. History would go on. Tribes, governments, and whole civilizations may rise and fall, trailing disaster in their wake, but I dared not confine my field of vision to the scenes of suffering around me. I needed to look up, to the stars.

"Can you bind the beautiful Pleiades? Can you loose the cords of Orion? Can you bring forth the constellations in the seasons or lead out the Bear with its cubs? Do you know the laws of the heavens? Can you set up God's dominion over the earth?" These questions God asked a man named Job who, obsessed with his own great pain, had confined his vision to the borders of his itchy skin. Remarkably, God's reminder seemed to help Job. His skin still itched, but Job got a glimpse of other matters God must attend to in a universe of 100 billion galaxies.

To me, God's speech in the book of Job conveys a tone of gruffness. But perhaps that is its most important message: the Lord of the universe has a right to gruffness when assailed by one tiny human being, notwithstanding the merits of his complaint. We descendants of Job dare not lose sight of The Big Picture, a sight best glimpsed on moonless, starry nights.

You can almost mark the advancement of a people by noting their interest in stargazing. Each great civilization of the past—Inca, Moghul, Chinese, Egyptian, Greek, Renaissance European—made major breakthroughs in astronomy. There is an irony at work in human history: One by one, civilizations gain the capacity to fathom their own insignificance, then fail to recognize that fact and fade away.

> Since that night, when I lay with warm sand at my back, the sky has never seemed so empty and the earth never as large.

What about us, we launchers of the Viking and Apollo spacecrafts, we makers of the orbiting Hubble observatory and the Very Large Array radio telescopes strewn over thirty-nine miles of New Mexico desert? Do our achievements make us more, or less, humble? More, or less, worshipful?

About the same time I read Chet Raymo, I went to see a film taken by a Space Shuttle crew with a special format Omnimax camera. The lightning storms impressed me most. Viewed from space, lightning flashes on and off in a random pattern of beauty, illuminating cloud cover several hundred miles wide at a burst. It flares, spreads across an expanse, glows, then pales. Most eerily, it makes no sound.

I was struck by the huge difference perspective makes. On earth, families huddled indoors, cars hid under highway overpasses, animals cowered in the forest, children cried out in the night. Transformers sparked, creeks flooded, dogs howled. But from space we saw only a soft, pleasant glow, enlarging then retreating, an ocean tide of light.

Chet Raymo, who sleeps in the day and stares upward at night, lives with a constant sense of wonder, a by-product of observing the universe.

He describes how the receding galaxies point back to a Big Bang of creation in which all the matter of the universe came into existence in a giant explosion that lasted one second. He acknowledges the unimaginable odds against anything good coming out of such an explosion by chance:

> If, one second after the Big Bang, the ratio of the density of the universe to its expansion rate had differed from its assumed value by only one part in 10^{15} (that's 1 followed by fifteen zeros), the universe would have either quickly collapsed upon itself or ballooned so rapidly that stars and galaxies could not have condensed from the primal matter. . . . If all the grains of sand on all the beaches of the Earth were possible universes— that is, universes consistent with the laws of physics as we know them—and only one of those grains of sand were a universe that allowed for the existence of intelligent life, then that one grain of sand is the universe we inhabit.

After reading Chet Raymo, I turned to a passage I had marked long ago in the extraordinary book *Alone*, Commander Richard Byrd's account of a six-month sojourn of solitude in Antarctica near the South Pole. Byrd often found himself looking up; all other landscape was blank white. Living farther south than any human being, he witnessed things in the sky—such as refraction phenomena that shot bands of color through the sun's core—visible to no one else on earth.

After one chilly afternoon stroll (it was 89° below zero in the season of perpetual night), Byrd sat down and wrote about what he had seen stargazing during many such walks.

> The conviction came that rhythm was too orderly, too harmonious, too perfect to be a product of blind chance—that, therefore, there must be purpose in the whole and that man was part of that whole and not an accidental offshoot. It was a

feeling that transcended reason; that went to the heart of man's despair and found it groundless. The universe was a cosmos, not a chaos; man was as rightfully a part of that cosmos as were the day, and night.

It takes great effort, and considerable faith, to keep The Big Picture in mind. In some ways it makes me feel utterly insignificant, in some ways eternally significant. If the God who engineered creation with such precision professes some whit of interest in what takes place on this speck of a planet, the least I can do is wander away from the streetlights more often, and look up.

25

CHAPTER 5

Of Whales and Polar Bears

Earth is crammed with heaven
And every bush aflame with God
But only those who see take off their shoes.
— ELIZABETH BARRETT BROWNING

I admit that I'm a soft touch for the Argument from Design. For me, the world of nature bears spectacular witness to the imaginative genius of our Creator. Consider these examples that I encountered on a trip to Alaska:

- A nearly invisible ice fish swims among the icebergs of Arctic and Antarctic waters, its survival made possible by the unique properties of its blood. A special protein acts as an antifreeze to keep ice crystals from forming, and its blood has no hemoglobin, or red pigment. As a result, the fish is virtually transparent.

- The instinctive navigational ability of common ducks, geese, and swans makes them the envy of the aircraft industry. On their trips south, some of the geese maintain a speed of fifty miles per hour, and fly 1,000 miles before making their first rest stop.

- When it comes to navigation, polar bears are no slouches either. A polar bear that is tranquilized, trapped, and released 300 miles away can usually find its way home, even across drift ice that changes constantly and holds no landmarks and few odors. But bears and birds are rank amateurs compared to lowly salmon, who cruise the expanse of the Pacific Ocean for several years before returning (by scent? magnetic field?) to the streams of their birth.

- Baby musk oxen are born in March and April, when temperatures still languish around 30° below zero. Thus, as the tiny musk ox drops two feet to the ground, its surrounding temperature drops 130°. The mother must hasten to lick blood and fluid from the coat of the steaming calf lest it freeze. Within a few minutes, the calf staggers to its feet and begins to nurse.

- Comparatively, grizzlies and polar bears have it easy. Ursine mothers feel no pain when giving birth for the simple reason that birthing takes place in the dead of winter, hibernation time. The cub struggles through the birth canal, pokes around the new world, and figures out the nursing process on its own. (Imagine the mother bear's surprise when spring rolls around.)

- One more fact about polar bears. For years it puzzled researchers that polar bears and harp seals never showed up on the aerial infrared photographs used in animal censuses. Yet both species showed up very dark on ultraviolet photographs, even though white objects normally reflect, rather than absorb, ultraviolet light rays. In 1978 a U.S. Army researcher discovered the reason. Polar bear hairs are not white at all, but transparent. Under a scanning electron microscope they appear as hollow tubes, without pigment. They act like tiny fiber-optic tubes, trapping the warming ultraviolet rays and funneling them to the bear's body. At the same time the fur provides such efficient insulation that the bear's outer temperature stays virtually the same as the surrounding ice— which explains why bears do not show up on infrared photos.

* * *

W hen I learn such details about the natural world, I feel like writing a hymn in honor of the polar bear or musk ox. Such a hymn would have good precedent: In his majestic speech at the end of the book of Job, God himself pointed to the wonders of creation as compelling proof of his power and wisdom. When he and Job compared résumés, Job ended up repenting in dust and ashes.

> For just that moment, nothing else—dinner reservations, the trip schedule, my life back in Chicago—mattered.

As I say, I'm a soft touch for the Argument from Design. Still, I must acknowledge that not everyone responds to nature in the same way. As novelist Walker Percy has observed, "There may be signs of [God's] existence, but they point both ways and are therefore ambiguous and so prove nothing. . . . The wonders of the universe do not convince those most conversant with the wonders, the scientists themselves."

Why isn't the Argument from Design more convincing? Percy is right: nature gives off mixed signals. I left Alaska with sentiments of worship and admiration; the polar bears' prey probably has a different perspective. And I might have been less anxious to write a hymn had I pondered instead the design of Alaskan mosquitoes or of the Cecidomyian gall midge (whose young hatch inside their mother and literally eat their way out, devouring the mother as they go).

Like humanity, the rest of the created world presents a strange mixture of beauty and horror, of splendid cooperation and savage competition. In the apostle Paul's words, "We know that the whole creation has been groaning as in the pains of childbirth right up to the present time" (Romans 8:22). Nature is our fallen sister, not our mother.

C. S. Lewis used to say that the Christian does not go to nature to learn theology—the message is too garbled—but rather to fill theological words with meaning: "Nature never taught me that there exists a God of glory and of infinite majesty. I had to learn that in other ways. But nature gave the word *glory* a meaning for me. I still do not know where else I could have found one."

I didn't learn much theology on my trip to Alaska. But wading in a glacial stream dyed red with spawning salmon, and watching a bald eagle pluck a sea bass out of the bay, I did fill a few words with meaning. Words like *joy* and *awe*.

Just a few miles outside Anchorage, as I drove along the oddly named inlet "Turnagain Arm," I noticed a number of cars pulled off the highway. When Alaskan cars pull over, that usually means animals. Against the slate-gray sky, the water of Turnagain Arm appeared to have a slight greenish cast, interrupted by small whitecaps. Soon I saw these were not whitecaps at all, but whales—silvery white beluga whales. A pod was feeding no more than fifty feet offshore.

I stood for forty minutes, listening to the rhythmic motion of the sea, following the graceful, ghostly crescents of surfacing whales. The crowd was hushed, even reverent. We passed around binoculars, saying nothing, simply watching. More cars pulled off the road. Dogs chased each other on the shoreline, their owners oblivious. For just that moment, nothing else—dinner reservations, the trip schedule, my life back in Chicago—mattered.

We were confronted with a scene of quiet beauty and a majesty of scale. We all felt small. We stood together in silence, until the whales moved farther out. And then we climbed the bank together and got in our cars to resume our busy, ordered lives that somehow seemed less urgent. And it wasn't even Sunday.

CHAPTER 6

Reading Genesis in the Wild

After thirteen years in downtown Chicago, my wife and I moved to a remote setting in the Rocky Mountains. I find myself missing the characters in our old neighborhood: the can collector who called himself Tut Uncommon, the mental patient who sat in a coffee shop all day pretending to smoke an unlit cigarette, the eccentric who roamed Clark Street with a sign that read, "I NEED A WIFE!"

In our new location, we see more animals than people. Elk graze on the hill behind our house, woodpeckers pound on the wood siding, and a red fox we've named Foster drops by every evening in search of handouts. The other day Foster sat outside the screen door and listened to an entire segment of *Prairie Home Companion* as I wallpapered my office. He cocked his head quizzically a few times during the bluegrass music, but all in all seemed to enjoy the show.

Not long after the move I began reading through the Bible, starting with Genesis, and soon discovered that the Bible takes on a different tone in new surroundings. I read the creation account during snow season. Mountains gleamed in the morning sunlight, and every Ponderosa pine wore a mantle of pure, crystalline white. It was easy to imagine the joy of original creation, a time when, as God later described to Job, "the morning stars sang together and all the angels shouted for joy."

That same week, however, a loud thump interrupted my reading. A small bird, a pine siskin with a notched tail and yellow chevron stripes on each wing, had crashed into the window. It lay stomach-down on a clump of snow, gasping for breath, with bright red drops of blood spilling from its beak. For twenty minutes it lay there, its head nodding as if in drowsiness, until finally it made one last fluttering effort to rise, then dropped its head into the snow and died.

As tragedies go, I had witnessed a minor one. On the noon news I heard of slaughter in Bosnia and bloodshed in Africa. Somehow, though, a single bird's death, enacted just across the windowpane, brought home the gravity of my reading for that day: it captured in miniature the chasmic change between Genesis 2 and 3, between paradise and fallen creation.

The author of Genesis was a master of understatement. A flat report, "Thus the heavens and the earth were completed in all their vast array" (Genesis 2:1), sums up the stupendous process that brought into being quasars and nebulae, blue whales and dwarf shrimp, penguins and pine siskins. Although presumably written long after the Fall, the first two chapters of Genesis give the merest hints of any tragedy to follow. "They felt no shame," the author says of naked Adam and Eve, a comment that makes sense only to readers acquainted with shame.

Genesis 2 includes another editorial comment as well, one I had never before noticed. In a remarkable scene, God parades the many animals before Adam "to see what he would name them." What a strange new sensation for omnipotence! The Creator of the universe in all its vast array assumes the role of Spectator, waiting "to see" what Adam would do.

We humans have been granted "the dignity of causation," said Blaise Pascal, and the next few chapters of Genesis prove causation to be both dignity and burden. In short order, human beings master the basics of family life, agriculture, music, and tool-making. But they also master the art of murder, fornication, and other deeds drearily characteristic of the species. Before long, God "regrets" his decision to create: "The LORD was grieved that he had made man on the earth, and his heart was filled with pain" (6:6).

Throughout the Old Testament, God seems to alternate between Spectator and Participant. At times, when blood cries out from the ground, when injustice grows intolerable, when evil overruns all constraints, God acts—decisively, even violently. Mountains smoke, the ground yawns open, people die. The New Testament, though, shows the God who selflessly shared the dignity of causation descending to become its Victim. He who had the right to destroy the world—and had nearly done so once in Noah's day—chose instead to love the world, at any cost.

> God seems to alternate between Spectator and Participant.

I sometimes wonder how hard it has been for God not to act in history. How must it feel to see the glories of creation—the rain forests, the whales, the elephants—obliterated one by one? How must it feel to see the Jews themselves nearly annihilated? To lose a Son? What is the cost of God's self-restraint?

I had always thought of the Fall in terms of its effect on us humans, namely, the penalties outlined in Genesis 3. This time I was struck by its effect on God. The Bible devotes only two chapters to the glories of original creation. All that follows describes the agonizing course of re-creation.

The Bible begins and ends with similar images. In Revelation the garden has been transformed into a city, but a river runs through it, and on each side of the river stands the tree of life. No angel with a flaming sword now guards the tree; its fruit abounds, and even its leaves help "the healing of the nations." Referring back to Genesis 3, Revelation sums up the new reality with these simple words: "No longer will there be any curse."

Reading Genesis in the Wild

We live out our days between memory and foretaste. The view out my window—whether it's of the Rocky Mountains or the characters on Clark Street—gives mere glimpses of what God had in mind in Genesis 1–2, and of what he has promised in Revelation 21–22. I stand in awe at the enormous effort required to restore what has been spoiled. All because God stepped back to see what Adam—what you and I—would do.

CHAPTER 7

Disturbing the Universe

D oubt, for me, tends to come in an overwhelming package, all at once. I don't worry much about nuances of particular doctrines, but every so often I catch myself wondering about the whole grand scheme of faith.

I stand in the futuristic terminal in Denver, for example, watching important-looking people in business suits, briefcases clutched to their sides like weapons, pause at an espresso bar before scurrying off to another concourse. *Do any of them ever think about God?* I wonder.

Christians share an odd belief in parallel universes. One universe consists of glass and steel and wool clothes and leather briefcases and the smell of freshly ground coffee. The other consists of angels and sinister spiritual forces and somewhere out there places called heaven and hell. We palpably inhabit the material world; it takes faith to consider ourselves citizens of the other, invisible world.

Occasionally the two worlds merge for me, and these rare moments are anchors for my faith. The time I snorkeled on a coral reef and suddenly the flashes of color and abstract design flitting around me became a window to a Creator who exults in life and beauty. The time my wife forgave me for something that did not merit forgiveness —that, too, became a window, allowing a startling glimpse of divine grace.

I have these moments, but soon toxic fumes from the material world seep in. Sex appeal! Power! Money! Military might! These are what matter most in life, I'm told, not the simpering platitudes of Jesus' teachings in the Sermon on the Mount. For me, living in a fallen world, doubt seems more like *forgetfulness* than disbelief.

Unlike most people, I do not feel much Dickensian nostalgia at Christmastime. The holiday fell just a few days after my father died early in my childhood, and all my memories of the season are darkened by the shadow of that sadness. For this reason, perhaps, I am rarely stirred by the sight of manger scenes and tinseled trees. Yet, more and more, Christmas has enlarged in meaning for me, primarily as an answer to my doubts, an antidote to my forgetfulness.

In Christmas, the two worlds come together. If you read the Bible alongside a Civilization 101 textbook, you will see how seldom that happens. The textbook dwells on the glories of ancient Egypt and the pyramids; the Bible's book of Exodus mentions the names of two Hebrew midwives but neglects to identify the Pharaoh. The textbook honors the contributions from Greece and Rome; the Bible contains a few scant references, mostly negative, and treats great civilizations as mere background static for God's work among the Jews.

Yet on Jesus the two books agree. I switched on my computer this morning and Microsoft Windows™ flashed the date, implicitly acknowledging what the Gospels and the history book both affirm: whatever you may believe about it, the birth of Jesus was so important that it split history into two parts. Everything that has ever happened on this planet falls into a category of before Christ or after Christ.

Why did Jesus come to earth? Theologians tend to answer that question from the human perspective: He came to show us what God is like, to show us what a human being should be like, to lay down his life as a sacrifice. I cannot help thinking, though, that Incarnation had meaning in other, cosmic ways.

God loves matter. You can read his signature everywhere: rocks that crack open to reveal delicate crystals, the clouds swirling around Venus, the fecundity of the oceans (home to 90 percent of all living things). Clearly, according to Genesis, the act of creation gave God pleasure.

Yet creation also introduced a gulf between God and his subjects, a gulf that can be sensed all through the Old Testament. Moses, David, Jeremiah, and other bold wrestlers with the Almighty flung this accusation to the heavens: "Lord, you don't know what it's like down here!" Job was most blunt: "Do you have eyes of flesh? Do you see as a mortal sees?"

> I, a citizen of the visible world, know well the struggle involved in clinging to belief in another, invisible world.

They had a point, a point God himself acknowledged with the decision to visit planet Earth. Choosing words that astonish, the author of Hebrews reflects on Jesus' life as a time when he "learned obedience," "was made perfect," and became a "sympathetic" high priest. There is only one way to learn sympathy, as signified by the Greek roots of the word, *syn pathos*, "to feel or suffer with."

Of the many reasons for Incarnation, surely one was to answer Job's accusation. *Do you have eyes of flesh?* Yes, indeed.

I, a citizen of the visible world, know well the struggle involved in clinging to belief in another, invisible world. Christmas turns the tables and hints at the struggle involved when the Lord of both worlds descends to live by the rules of the one. In Bethlehem, the two worlds came together, realigned; what Jesus went on to accomplish on planet Earth made it possible for God someday to resolve all disharmonies in both worlds. No wonder a choir of angels broke out in spontaneous song, disturbing not only a few shepherds but the entire universe.

Disturbing the Universe

PART TWO

Finding
GOD
on the
Job

CHAPTER 8

They Also Serve Who Only Sit and Click

D uring the years we lived in Chicago, my wife directed a senior citizens' program among the very poor. A typical dinner-table conversation in our house went like this:

"How was your day, Janet?"

"Rough. I met a homeless family who'd been living in Lincoln Park and hadn't eaten in three days. After taking care of them I learned that eighty-nine-year-old Peg Martin had died. And then I discovered some gang members had broken into the church van and spray-painted graffiti all over it."

After filling in the details of those adventures, Janet would ask about my day. "Uh, let me think. What did happen today? I stared at a computer screen all day. Oh yeah—I found a very good adverb!"

Our daily routines, not to mention our personalities, could hardly differ more. Janet, vivacious, outgoing, gregarious, worked out of an office on Hill Street, the seamy locale made famous by the TV show *Hill Street Blues*. Her days were full of adventure, and full of people: often she served meals to seventy people at a time, and nearly every day she dealt with several dozen clients.

After we moved to Colorado, she began working in a hospice. The average patient admitted there dies within ten days. Janet now comes home with stories of families who have differing responses of courage, rage, or despair, but all are marked by the passion that grief compels.

Meanwhile, whether in Chicago or Colorado, I sit at home in my basement office staring at a flickering computer screen in search of the perfect word. (So far, computers only process words, they don't compose them.) The main "event" in my day occurs around noon, when the mailman arrives. Occasionally the telephone rings. And once a week or so I may meet someone for lunch. The daily regimen of a writer is not what you'd call glamorous.

You cannot imagine the vicarious thrill I felt when I first came across Philip Roth's description of writing in *The Ghost Writer:*

> I turn sentences around. That's my life. I write a sentence and then I turn it around. Then I look at it and I turn it around again. Then I have lunch. Then I come back in and write another sentence. Then I have tea and turn the new sentence around. Then I read the two sentences over and turn them both around. Then I lie down on my sofa and think. Then I get up and throw them out and start from the beginning.

He has described my life precisely. The vast difference between that sort of life and my wife's used to bother me. Following my usual course of introspection and self-doubt, I would tend to discount my own work and accept blame for not having a more direct impact on people. "Janet puts into practice what I write about," I would say, only half-joking, to friends. I left unstated the clear implication that what I did was somehow less valuable, less worthy.

I suppose I encounter my own version of the lonely housewife syndrome: sitting home all day, with such a narrow focus, I have trouble imagining that my daily routine makes much difference to the world or anyone in it. Yes, I get mail from readers, but such letters come long after the act of writing, and the impact they describe is very indirect and vicarious. I observe no immediate results comparable to those of my wife, who can watch the actual facial expressions change on a hungry person fed, a homeless person sheltered, a grieving person comforted.

In addition, Janet comes home with stories so rich in fascinating detail as to make any writer drool. I remember her visiting a lady named Beulah in the hospital, for example. Beulah was born in 1892 to a wet nurse on a Louisiana plantation. Her mother, freed from slavery long before, had stayed on the plantation, and Beulah grew up playing under the front porch with the rich white children. Later, Beulah got bounced around from the plantation to New Orleans to Tennessee to Chicago. She had lived seventy-two years before Congress ever got around to the first Civil Rights Bill!

> What did happen today? Oh yeah—I found a very good adverb.

That night Janet came home full of stories Beulah had dredged up from her childhood days along the levees of the Mississippi River. World War I or II, the Great Depression, the Russian Revolution—you name a major event of the twentieth century and Beulah can resurrect a story about it.

I listen to such stories and think to myself, *If I could have Janet's job, I'd never experience writer's block again.* But then sober reality sets in to self-correct my fantasies. *There are two problems, Philip: First, you'd be terrible at Janet's job, and second, you'd have no time left over to write.* And so the next morning, after eating my cereal, I head downstairs to spend another day making the sound of insect clicks on my computer keyboard.

Over time, I have come to see that the very differences between us— in personality, outlook, and daily routine—actually represent a great strength. Janet provides me with a new set of eyes into a world I barely know about. I find challenge there, and stimulation. My own faith is tested as I hear of her attempts to bring hope to the lives of those who have so little. Sometimes, like now, her experiences even edge their way into my writing.

On the other hand, I can offer Janet calmness, reflection, and balance. I try to make our home a haven: a place for her to lick wounds, to gain perspective, to recharge for the next day's battles. (Again, the reverse housewife syndrome—is this not what women offered their career husbands for centuries?)

The New Testament frequently uses the image of a human body to illustrate the church. A body composed of many members with many gifts can accomplish far more than a one-celled organism. Individual cells may suffer an apparent "disadvantage": a human eye cell, for example, never gets to experience touch, or hearing, or anything at all but vision. But because of its specialization, that eye cell can contribute a wholly new level of sight. One-celled amoebas can see enough to galumph away from light, but that's about it.

I have found the same principle applies to marriage as well. I no longer view Janet's work with a sense of competition. Rather, I marvel at the differences in temperament and spiritual gifts that allow her to spend her day dealing with situations that would probably drive me crazy. I have learned to take pride in her work, to see it as a part of my own service to God. By serving her, and offering a listening ear, I can strengthen her and thus help assure that her vital work will continue.

On good days, I remember this principle, pray for Janet, and look for ways to help equip her for her demanding and wonderful—even holy—work. As for bad days—well, you'll probably find me sitting in front of a computer screen, looking a little cross-eyed, daydreaming of the great novels I could write if I spent my time on Hill Street instead of in my basement.

CHAPTER 9

The Power of Writing

I n a scene from the movie *Black Robe*, a Jesuit missionary tries to persuade a Huron chief to let him teach the tribe to read and write. The chief sees no benefit to this practice of scratching marks on paper until the Jesuit gives him a demonstration. "Tell me something I do not know," he says. The chief thinks for a moment and replies, "My woman's mother died in snow last winter."

The Jesuit writes a sentence and walks a few yards over to his colleague, who glances at it and then says to the chief, "Your mother-in-law died in a snowstorm?" The chief jumps back in alarm. He has just encountered the magical power of writing, which allows knowledge to leap across space and travel in silence through symbols.

Augustine's *Confessions* gives a wonderful glimpse of Saint Ambrose, who had mastered the art of reading silently, without moving his lips. Augustine and his friends would gather to watch this feat, amazed that Ambrose could comprehend and retain the unpronounced words, as if by telepathy. Until the thirteenth century, in fact, very few people could read in such a novel way. (Mastery of such practice, interestingly, led to a surge in private prayer: until then believers viewed both prayer and reading as group activities.)

I once read a long and at times tedious study called *The History and Power of Writing*, by Henri-Jean Martin, which sets out many examples of writing's impact on the world. Most of history has viewed writing as a

45

supplement to the more reliable medium of oral communication. Scholars recorded epic poems or lists of facts as an aid to memory, but rarely used writing to communicate new ideas. For the epic poets, writing proved entirely too constraining: No longer could they play to the audience by adding embellishment to the recitations. Indeed, stripped of inflection and facial expression, detached from the sensory surroundings of the campfire or banquet hall, incapable of dialogue, writing seemed a thin, frail medium.

The church has had a love/hate relationship with writing, even though it was invented as a way to record truths about the sacred. (Druids resisted writing for this reason—they didn't want their secrets to get out.) Clerics led the way in bringing literacy to Europe, and during the Dark Ages, monasteries preserved the classics while society crumbled around them.

Yet through its book burnings, censorship, and persecution of authors, the church also tried to control writing. Such controls fell apart during the Protestant Reformation, which happened to coincide with the invention of the printing press. Reformers saw writing as a freedom-enhancing medium. By translating the Bible and other books into vernacular language, and distributing them widely, they could free doctrine from the thought-police of the church hierarchy. Soon, of course, Protestant thought-police emerged, too, but with less effect: the word had been irretrievably set free.

R eading Henri-Jean Martin's book on the history of writing, I could not help reflecting on my own pilgrimage. I grew up in a southern fundamentalist church that taught blatant racism, apocalyptic fear of Communism, and America-first patriotism. Christian doctrine was dished out in a "believe and don't ask questions" style, laced with fervid emotionalism.

For me, reading opened a chink of light that became a window to another world. I remember the impact of a mild book like *To Kill a Mock-*

ingbird, which called into question the apartheid assumptions of my friends and neighbors. Later, reading books like *Black Like Me, The Autobiography of Malcolm X,* and Martin Luther King, Jr.'s *Letter from Birmingham City Jail*, I felt my whole world shatter. Like the startled Huron chief, I, too, experienced the power that allowed one human mind to penetrate another with no intermediary but a piece of flattened wood pulp.

I especially came to value the freedom-enhancing aspect of writing. Speakers in the churches I attended could RAISE THEIR VOICES! and play emotions like musical instruments. But alone in my room, voting with every turn of the page, I met other representatives of the kingdom of God—C. S. Lewis, G. K. Chesterton, Saint Augustine—whose calmer voices leapt across time to convince me that somewhere Christians lived who knew grace as well as law, love as well as judgment, reason as well as passion.

> I saw that spoiled words, their original meaning wrung out, could be reclaimed.

I became a writer, I believe, because of my own experience of the power of words. I saw that spoiled words, their original meaning wrung out, could be reclaimed. I saw that writing could penetrate into the crevices, bringing spiritual oxygen to people trapped in airtight boxes. I saw that when God conveyed to us the essence of his self-expression, God called it the Word. The Word comes in the most freedom-enhancing way imaginable.

I feel both proud and ashamed of my profession. We have at times used words like clubs, not levers. We have used words to enslave, not liberate. Even so, somehow the written word has endured. I think of Irish monks laboring for weeks, even months, over single letters of illuminated manuscripts, keeping the word alive in an age when few people could read, or cared to. I think of faithful writers like Solzhenitsyn who relied on the *samizdat* press to distribute hand-typed sheaves of witness from hand to hand.

We may be entering a different kind of Dark Ages, a time when the devil owns the airwaves and when words seem gray and dull compared to the dazzle of virtual reality and multimedia CD-ROM. I have hope, though. Despite the waves of hysteria and authoritarianism in church history, words of truth have survived and emerged later as living forces to change individuals and entire cultures. I have experienced their power. I pray that the church, in increasingly oppressive times, will remember that words have their greatest impact when they enhance freedom, when they liberate.

48

CHAPTER 10

The Never-Never Land of Religious Media

B ecause I spend so much of my life alone in a basement office, when I do emerge outdoors I sometimes feel like a mole blinking in the light. Never was this more true than when I agreed to do an author's media tour. For several weeks I visited television and radio stations as part of a campaign to introduce my book *Disappointment with God*.

I knew I was in trouble the very first day, in Dallas, when a radio station booked me on a talk show with a Christian comedian. An expert at mouth sounds and hand sounds, he could precisely duplicate the noises made by barnyard animals, race cars, and train wrecks. Between the two of us, we covered the bases: he could do a perfect imitation of a jet plane taking off, and I could try to explain why God allows airplanes to crash. Why did I feel like a character in an absurdist play?

From there I drove to a Baptist television station to field phone calls on a televised counseling show. The program was exceptionally well run, but not without its strange aspects. The topic "disappointment with God" attracted callers with wrenching personal stories: child abuse, alcoholism, cancer, AIDS, you name it. As these callers spilled out their traumas over staticky phone lines, I could only stare into a camera and nod sympathetically. Meanwhile in my peripheral vision, the show's producers were running around holding up large placards: "This man's a crank. Get him off the air!" and "Wind it up fast! Thirty seconds to commercial break!"

In Los Angeles I spent three hours and fifty minutes in helpless agitation on a gridlocked freeway, listening to the radio program I was supposed to be on. "We know you're out there on the freeway, Philip," the gracious host said over the air. "Just drive carefully. Don't worry." I did drive carefully—could I do otherwise at five miles per hour? I also worried, and with good reason: I never made it to the show.

In San Francisco I appeared on the same program with a former Las Vegas showgirl who was now spearheading an effort to build a sixty-story prayer tower in the shape of a cross in every major U.S. city. She had been converted through a near-death experience on the operating table. "My career was suffering so I had to get my busts enlarged again," she said. While she lay anesthetized, an angel escorted her to hell, where she saw an eighteen-wheeler composed entirely of human flesh—"Even the mud flaps were made of flesh!"—dumping America's teenagers into a molten lake. Now I ask you, how can any work of popular theology compete on a program with stories like that?

My media tour ended at Heritage USA, the vestigial organization that survived the fall of Jim and Tammy Faye Bakker. I had visited the grounds twice before, once in the Bakkers' heyday and once during the more somber reign of Jerry Falwell. The mood this time was palpably different. The central cluster of Disneylandish buildings glowed out of the darkness like Las Vegas after a neutron bomb. There were many buildings in this phantom city, but no people. All exuberance was gone. Condominiums were shuttered, construction cranes stood idle, the water slide was dry. I went on an eerie jog along the Walk of Faith, marked with bronze plaques inscribed with slogans of prosperity and faith. The television ministry, however, was still limping along, operated by a skeleton crew under the supervision of a bankruptcy court.

Thinking back on my previous visits, I noticed the biggest change in the staff members themselves. Many had been hired by the Bakkers, whom they had lionized, but had gradually become disillusioned by the shocking revelations of wrongdoing. The remnant who stayed on did so because they truly believed in the ministry. They seemed humble, genuine, broken. They seemed Christian.

After three weeks of such experiences in the never-never land of religious media, I came up with some subjective, unscientific observations:

> As callers spilled out their traumas over staticky phone lines, I could only stare into a camera and nod sympathetically.

1. Christian television stations hire a disproportionate number of beautiful women who wear their hair and their dresses long. Most of these have southern accents.

2. At least half the time, the interview host first sets eyes on a guest author's book five minutes before the interview program.

3. Charismatic stations can't figure out why anyone would want to write a book on disappointment with God.

4. Of the programs I visited, those run by Southern Baptists and Seventh-Day Adventists were the best organized, with their hosts most eager for a conversation of substance. (But try to get a good cup of coffee at a Seventh-Day Adventist studio!)

5. On secular stations, callers were obsessed with one question: "How can a loving God permit so much suffering?" On Christian stations, the callers were obsessed with the opposite: "Yes, God directly causes suffering, and here's why. . . ."

It took a while for me to adjust to the built-in *artificiality* of the media. In normal life you determine how you're relating to the rest of the world by attending to such clues as body language and eye contact. If you're speaking before a group and everyone looks close-eyed and slack-jawed, you surmise you're not communicating well. But the television and radio audience, of course, remains invisible. Is anyone paying attention? You can't tell. In the television studio itself, the hosts/hostesses only bother to act interested in what you're saying when the camera angle includes them. Otherwise, they may be studying the next question, whispering to the producer, primping in a mirror, straightening a tie.

The call-in format, increasingly popular, introduces a new level of artificiality. I learned quickly why politicians rely on "sound bites." The message must adapt to the medium, not vice versa. When a woman called in, sobbing, to tell me her lifelong story of unrelieved tragedy, I could hardly say, "I'm sorry, but there's not a thing I could tell you in the next ninety seconds to fix a deep-rooted problem like that." Instead, I searched for a capsule summary, some insight that even in abbreviated form might offer a new perspective or simply give hope. Ninety seconds later, we cut to a commercial and I never heard from the woman again.

Sometimes the callers would preface their stories with the statement, "I've never told this to anyone before." It was a frightening disclosure, one that gets to the heart of the central strength—and weakness—of religious broadcasting: some of these people had a closer relationship with their television sets than with any living human being.

Abraham, Jesus, and Muhammad in New Orleans

Occasionally I also get invited to unusual gatherings as a result of my writing. One of the most memorable took place in New Orleans at the invitation of M. Scott Peck, psychiatrist and author of such books as *The Road Less Traveled* and *People of the Lie*. Peck has a theory that the process of building community must precede the resolution of disagreements, and he brought together thirty disparate people in order to test that theory.

53

Peck convened ten Jews, ten Christians, and ten Muslims, a microcosm representing perhaps the most fractious disagreement of Western civilization. The central issue that shadowed us was, "Can people with fundamentally different truth claims live together without killing each other?" We met at a Catholic retreat center the weekend before Mardi Gras. (Try explaining the Christian roots of that booze-and-sex bash to followers of another religion.) For three days we discussed, well, whatever we wanted to discuss.

Certain cultural differences surfaced right away. Scott Peck conducts his community-building workshops according to a formula that calls for introspective "I" statements and personal sharing, and the Jews responded warmly to this approach. "Don't forget, we invented psychotherapy," joked one rabbi. Muslim participants, though, showed little enthusiasm. One imam tried to explain, "We have a cultural aversion to psychotherapy. You'll rarely hear a Muslim talk about personal problems. It just isn't done."

As a result, we Christians frequently found ourselves on the sidelines watching Muslims respond to the Jews' self-questioning musings with fixed pronouncements of absolute truth. These in turn provoked even more "I" statements from the Jews and more pronouncements from the Muslims. It felt good to be on the sidelines, actually; Christians don't have a very good history with either of these religions, and I much preferred our new mediator role to past pogroms and Crusades.

I learned a new word in New Orleans, supersessionism, which helped me understand the Muslims' apparent aplomb. The Jews resented the notion that Christian faith had *superseded* Judaism. "I feel like a curiosity of history, as if my religion should be put in a nursing home," said one. "It grates on me to hear the term *Old Testament God* or even the word *Old* Testament, for that matter." I had to agree that Christianity has a frankly supersessionist aspect. Jesus introduced the "new covenant" even as he transformed Jewish Passover Seder into what Christians now call "the Lord's Supper." Later, the apostle Paul referred to the Old Testament Law as a "tutor" or "schoolmaster" to lead us to Christ.

I had not realized, however, that Muslims look on both faiths with a supersessionist attitude. As they see it, just as Christianity grew out of and incorporated parts of Judaism, Islam grew out of and incorporated parts of both religions. Abraham was a prophet; Jesus was a prophet; but Muhammad was The Prophet. The Old Testament has a place, as does the New Testament, but the Koran is "the final revelation." Hearing my own faith talked about with such condescension gave me insight into how Jews have felt for two millennia.

Ironically, it was the common language of pain that seemed to bring the three groups together. Many of the Jewish participants had lost family members in the Holocaust, and some had also served as volunteers in Israel's wars against Arab neighbors. On the Muslim side, one woman told of the horrors that descended upon her once-lovely neighborhood in Beirut, Lebanon. Another Muslim gave a wrenching account of the Deir Yassin massacre in 1948, when members of the Israeli Stern gang killed 250 members of his village and threw their bodies in a well. He, at the age of ten, was fleet enough to escape. But a soldier shot his two-year-old brother and ninety-six-year-old grandmother in cold blood.

Suffering sometimes serves as a moat and sometimes as a bridge. The Muslim who fled from the soldiers at Deir Yassin years later had an automobile accident in the United States. It was a Jewish nurse who stopped, tied a tourniquet with her scented hanky, and painstakingly plucked glass from his face. He believes she saved his life. The Muslim man's wife, a physician, went on to say that she had once treated a patient with a strange tattoo on his wrist. When she asked about it, he told her about the Holocaust, a historical event omitted from her high school, college, and graduate school education in Arab countries. For the first time, she understood Jewish pain.

> Our meeting in
> New Orleans
> did not change the
> Middle East equation.
> But it did change us.

Why do human beings keep doing it to each other? Yugoslavia, Ireland, Sudan, the West Bank—is there no end to the cycle of pain fueled by religion? As Gandhi observed, the logic of "an eye for an eye, a tooth for a tooth" cannot sustain itself forever; ultimately both parties end up blind and toothless.

Our meeting in New Orleans did not, rest assured, change the Middle East equation, or make peace between three major religions any more likely. But it did change us. For once we focused on intersections and connections, not just boundaries. We got to know Hillel, Dawud, and Bob, human faces behind the labels Jew, Muslim, and Christian.

Abraham, Jesus, and Muhammad in New Orleans

Each faith held a worship service—Jews on Friday, Muslims on Saturday, Christians on Sunday—to which the others were invited as observers. The Jewish service consisted of readings from Psalms and the Torah and some warm-hearted singing. The Muslim worship service consisted mostly of reverential prayers to the Almighty. We Christians celebrated the Lord's Supper, and told of how it helps us to look back to Christ's death, to look forward to his return, and to live in the present, a state of grace made possible by his body, broken for us.

All three services had striking similarities, and reminded us how much the three faiths have in common. Perhaps the intensity of feeling among the three traditions stems from a common heritage: family disputes are always the stubbornest, and civil wars the bloodiest.

One rabbi gave this response to the weekend: "I did not want to come here. I almost canceled. Ten days ago I was visiting Auschwitz. I stood where so many thousands died—just for the crime of being Jewish. At Auschwitz, some Catholics asked me to pray with them. How could I? I knew that the Catholic church had remained silent while members of my family were forced to dig their own graves.

"I wasn't ready to meet with Christians and Muslims so soon. I could not get past my own pain. This weekend has been hard for me, and yet now I can say I am glad I came. It was the pain of healing I have felt, not the pain of fresh wounds.

"A few of us have now heard each other's stories. We have been affected. Yet the institutions we represent keep on hating, keep on murdering. Can what happens this weekend produce anything more than a beautiful experience for the few of us who have gathered? Is there any way for the systems themselves to change, any way to break the cycle?"

The rabbi had circled back to the summary question of the weekend: "Can people with fundamentally different truth claims live together without killing each other?" That, sadly, is a question that cannot be answered by one weekend in New Orleans.

CHAPTER 12

Career Dividends

I have written three books with Dr. Paul Brand, a missionary surgeon and leprosy specialist who has lived his life in almost equal thirds: one-third in England, one-third in India, and one-third in the United States. Writers are parasites—we leach life from other people—and I will always be grateful for the opportunity to have had some share, albeit vicarious, in this extraordinary life. Dr. Brand was approaching eighty when I helped write his memoirs *(Pain: The Gift Nobody Wants)*, and I traveled to India and England in search of the forces that shaped him. "Please," his daughter once urged me, "help make some sense out of the happy jumble of my father's life and thoughts."

In India we were welcomed like visiting royalty. As we approached Brand's boyhood home, a throng of people rushed down the hillside to meet our vehicle. Women, colorful as tropical birds in their bright saris, draped floral leis around our necks and led us to a feast spread on banana leaves. After the meal a hundred people gathered in the chapel (handbuilt by Brand's father) and treated us to an hour-long program of hymns, tributes, and ceremonial dances.

Our reception in individual homes made an even deeper impression on me. One man, Namo, had a twenty-year-old photo of Dr. Brand on his wall, captioned "May the Spirit that is in him live in me." When Namo told me his story, I could easily understand the affection he feels for his former surgeon.

As a youth Namo had to leave university in the middle of his final year; telltale patches of leprosy had appeared on his skin, and his hand was retracting into a rigid claw position. Rejected by his school, his village, and finally his family, Namo made his way to a leprosarium in southern India where a young doctor was trying out some experimental hand surgery techniques. There were three million people with leprosy in India, and twelve million worldwide, but Brand was the first orthopedic surgeon to attempt to treat their deformities.

Namo recalled that dark day: "I was so angry at my condition I could hardly speak. Stuttering, I told Dr. Brand my hands were now useless to me. Soon my feet would be, too. For all I cared, he could cut them off." Namo made a slashing motion with one hand across his other wrist. "Anyway, he could do anything he wanted if he thought he might learn something."

Fortunately, Namo was wrong about his prognosis. Drugs halted the spread of the disease. And after undergoing a painstaking series of surgical procedures over a five-year period, he regained the use of his hands and feet. He took training in physiotherapy, began working with other leprosy patients, and went on to become Chief of Physical Therapy at the All-India Institute.

Later that day I visited Sadan, another of Brand's former patients. He looked like a miniature version of Gandhi: skinny, balding, perched cross-legged on the edge of a bed. In a high-pitched, singsong voice he told me wrenching stories of past rejection: the classmates who made fun of him in school, the driver who kicked him—literally, with his shoe—off a public bus, the many employers who refused to hire him despite his training and talent, the hospitals that turned him away.

"When I got to Vellore, I spent the night on the Brands' verandah, because I had nowhere else to go," said Sadan. "That was unheard of for a person with leprosy back then. I can still remember when Dr. Brand took my infected, ulcerated feet in his hands. I had been to many doctors. A few had examined my hands and feet from a distance, but Dr. Brand and his wife were the first medical workers who dared to touch me. I had nearly forgotten what human touch felt like."

Sadan then recounted the elaborate sequence of medical procedures—tendon transfers, nerve strippings, toe amputations, and cataract removal—performed by Dr. Brand and his ophthalmologist wife. He spoke for half an hour. His past life was a catalogue of human suffering.

But as we sipped our last cup of tea in his home, just before leaving to catch a plane to England, Sadan made this astonishing statement: "Still, I must say that I am now happy that I had this disease."

"Happy?" I asked, incredulous.

"Yes," replied Sadan. "Apart from leprosy, I would have been a normal man with a normal family, chasing wealth and a higher position in society. I would never have known such wonderful people as Dr. Paul and Dr. Margaret, and I would never have known the God who lives in them."

> Whether we live out our days in India, England, or Clarkston, Georgia, the true measure of our worth will not depend on a curriculum vitae or an income statement.

Our reception in England made for a striking contrast. There, too, Dr. Brand and I retraced the steps of his past, visiting the ancestral home where his missionary parents had spent their furloughs, standing on the hospital roof where as a medical resident he had fire-watched during the Blitz, touring the Royal College of Surgeons where he had delivered two prestigious Hunterian lectures. But no one garlanded us with leis and no one gathered around us to sing hymns and give testimonials.

In the setting of his early medical adventures, Dr. Brand seemed, if anything, an anachronism. We wandered from receptionist to receptionist at University College Hospital inquiring after former faculty colleagues. "Who? Could you spell that name?" was the typical response. Finally, in a darkened hallway, we found a row of photos of some of Brand's teachers—doctors who were as famous in their day as Christiaan Barnard and C. Everett Koop are in ours.

Career Dividends

I caught myself wondering how Paul Brand's career might have played itself out had he stayed in London. Even working in a remote Indian village among outcast leprosy patients, he had achieved a measure of renown: an Albert Lasker award, a chapter in most manuals of hand surgery, the highest possible award from the U.S. Public Health Service, a Commander of the British Empire medal from the queen, several surgical procedures named after him. If he had stayed in a research capacity at a well-equipped laboratory, who knows what honors might have come his way. A Nobel Prize perhaps?

But what then? His picture would join the others in the darkened hallway, now dusty and beginning to yellow. His name, like theirs, would appear as a footnote in the medical textbooks. Fame in the annals of medicine rarely lasts long; microsurgery techniques have already outdated most of the procedures considered breakthroughs in Brand's youth. In contrast, his "sacrificial" work as a missionary surgeon in India continues to bear fruit, in the transformed lives of Namo and Sadan and hundreds like them.

Coming so close together, the encounters in India and England became for me a kind of parable contrasting the transience of fame with the permanence of investing in service to others. Whether we live out our days in India, England, or Clarkston, Georgia, the true measure of our worth will depend not on a curriculum vitae or an income statement, but on the spirit we pass on to others.

"Whoever finds his life will lose it, and whoever loses his life for my sake will find it," said Jesus in his proverb most often repeated in the Gospels. Each career path offers its own rewards. But after sitting with Dr. Brand in the homes of Namo and Sadan, and then touring the Hall of Fame at the Royal College of Surgeons, I had no doubt about which rewards truly last.

CHAPTER 13

Legacy of the Jolly Jester

I will always associate my only serious diet with the author and journalist G. K. Chesterton. First, a word about the diet. I hardly qualified as overweight, but shortly after my fortieth birthday an unauthorized thirteen pounds suddenly appeared on my body and I determined to do something about it.

My friends, especially those truly overweight, showed no sympathy whatever: "A diet, huh? Are you trying to lose or gain weight?" Very funny. As for me, I felt offended that my body would take it upon itself to enlarge without prior consultation.

The diet worked, I'm happy to say, and after my proper physical shape had reasserted itself, I could reflect philosophically on what I had learned. Mainly, I realized that I had long borne a ponderous prejudice against fat people. Never having had to battle weight problems, I felt little compassion for those who do.

During my diet, I happened to be reading Chesterton, whose most famous works were penned during the first decades of this century, and I often found myself thinking about him. As far as I know, that extraordinary English gentleman never attempted a diet, and as a result his weight hovered just under the three-hundred-pound mark. His girth and general poor health disqualified him from military service, a fact that led to a rather brusque encounter with a patriot during World War I. "Why aren't you out at the front?" demanded the indignant young lady when she spied Chesterton on the streets of London. He coolly replied, "My dear madam, if you will step round this way a little, you will see that I *am.*"

That distinctive shape made Chesterton a favorite of London caricaturists. It took only a few strokes for a skilled cartoonist to capture his essence: from the side he looked like a giant capital *P*. Chesterton rounded out his reputation with other eccentricities, most of which perfectly fulfilled the stereotype of a slovenly, absent-minded professor. For example, here is a biographer's account of a public debate with George Bernard Shaw:

> In all their debates Chesterton never did become the smooth and polished orator that Shaw was. He usually arrived late, made comments about his size (by 1911 he weighed 270 pounds), and carried a bunch of scribbled notes on odd bits of paper, at which he would peer nearsightedly. Bending his head to look at them, he muffled his high-pitched voice and his pince-nez fell off. He blew through his moustache and chuckled amiably at his own wit. By contrast, Shaw was punctual and well-organized, a lean, dapper man with a gorgeous Irish voice and the gestures of an accomplished actor. (From *The Outline of Sanity* by Alzina Stone Dale)

We miss Chesterton today, I think. For all his personal quirkiness, he managed to propound the Christian faith with as much wit, good humor, and sheer intellectual force as anyone in this century. With the zeal of a knight defending the last redoubt he took on, in person and in print, Shaw, H. G. Wells, Sigmund Freud, and anyone else who dared interpret the world apart from God and Incarnation. (Imagine a time when a debate on faith could fill a lecture hall!)

In his day, sober-minded modernists were seeking a new unified theory to explain the past and give hope to the future. Shaw, seeing history as a struggle between the classes, proposed a remedy of socialist utopianism. Wells interpreted the past as an evolutionary march toward progress and enlightenment (a view the rest of the century would do much to refute). Freud held up a vision of humanity free of repression and the bondage of the subconscious.

Ironically, all three of these progressives had in common a rather stern countenance. With furrowed brows and dark, haunted eyes they would expostulate on their optimistic visions of the future. Meanwhile, with a twinkle in his eye, laughing at his own jokes, Chesterton would cheerfully defend such "reactionary" concepts as original sin and the Last Judgment. In the public debates, typically he would charm the audience over to his side, then celebrate by hosting his chastened opponent at the nearest pub. Chesterton seemed to sense instinctively that a stern prophet will rarely break through to a society full of religion's "cultured despisers"; he preferred the role of jester.

> I fear that we have unconsciously accepted the model of "hard, cold, thin people" as the Christian personality ideal.

We direly need another Chesterton. In a time when culture and faith have drifted even farther apart, we could use his brilliance, his entertaining style, and above all his generous and joyful spirit. When society becomes polarized, as ours has, it is as if the two sides stand across a great divide and shout at each other. Chesterton had another approach: he walked to the center of a swinging bridge, roared a challenge to any single combat warriors, and then made both sides laugh aloud.

Chesterton claimed to distrust "hard, cold, thin people," and perhaps that's why I kept thinking of the jolly fat apologist during my diet. The personality types have reversed. Nowadays in the church sobermindedness has won the day. Theologians with long faces lecture on "the imperatives of the faith." The Religious Right warns of a holocaust of abortion and euthanasia. The religious left warns of holocausts nuclear and environmental. Heads of Christian relief agencies (a surprising number of whom, oddly, are overweight) report somberly on world hunger and overpopulation.

And I, writing in isolation from my basement, go on a crash diet to shed thirteen pounds. *Thirteen!* Chesterton could gain that much from an evening meal. I think of Shakespeare's words from *Julius Caesar:* "Let me have men about me that are fat, sleek-headed men, and such as sleep o' nights. Yond Cassius has a lean and hungry look. . . . Such men are dangerous."

Don't get me wrong. I know that gluttony used to be one of the seven deadly sins, and that obesity involves health risks comparable to those from smoking and drinking. What troubles me, though, is whether we have unconsciously accepted the model of "hard, cold, thin people" as the Christian personality ideal.

I sometimes wish the Bible had included more physical descriptions of its characters. I envision the apostle Paul as thin (too much prison gruel), and a little on the cold side. But what of Jeremiah? Have we reason to believe that a prophet who exercised so little emotional control would strictly regulate his appetite? Or what of King Solomon, who spread his table with foreign delicacies? I imagine the people in the Bible manifested the same range of personality types and physical shapes as one might find in the average bus depot today.

I don't regret going on my first diet. But I did learn, thanks mainly to G. K. Chesterton, that there is more to life than being thin. I realized that too easily my faith can become a tight-lipped, grim exercise of spiritual discipline, a blending of asceticism and rationalism. "Despair," Chesterton once said, "does not lie in being weary of suffering, but in being weary of joy." With all his excess, Chesterton never wearied of joy.

My diet goals successfully met, I'm left with one nagging question: Is it possible to be a soft, warm, thin person?

FINDING GOD in Unexpected PLACES

PART THREE

Finding GOD in a Fractured Society

CHAPTER 14

Eccentric on the Front Lines

H is breath reeking of alcohol, a grizzled, rheumy-eyed old man wearing a torn high school letter jacket sticks out his hand and slurs through a monologue about his needing bus money. His story sounds cockamamie, and your street wisdom tells you where a donation would likely go. Maybe you should offer to take him to a restaurant or to a rescue mission. But you don't. You shake your head, thrust your hands into your pockets, and keep walking.

You bump into people like him whenever you go downtown. Inside, it nags at you. Mother Teresa or John Wesley or Dwight L. Moody would not walk away. They'd do something about the man, even if it meant founding a ministry to take care of needs like his. "The face of Jesus in most distressing disguise," Mother Teresa once called the beggars of Calcutta. She got that right. Most distressing indeed.

By the end of the day, rationalization has papered over any lingering guilt. After all, you had important business to tend to. You can't possibly respond to all human needs. And other people specialize in ministries to street people—maybe you'll contribute some money to them.

Even so, you wonder. What would it would look like if a Christian took literally Jesus' sweeping commands and acted on them? What would a Good Samaritan look like today in urban America?

* * *

Such a person might look like Louise Adamson, a friend in Atlanta has told you. She's a missionary, but unlike any missionary you may have met before. She is more like a full-time Good Samaritan. You must meet her, he says. And so you do meet her, in a cramped office of an aging Presbyterian church in the shadow of a baseball stadium slated for demolition.

The furniture is government-issue hand-me-down. The carpet smells like the scrapings off the soles of thirty years' worth of shoes. Louise is in her sixties, you reckon. She has an ample nose, strong, straight teeth, a pitted complexion, a full head of graying hair. She is wearing a simple purple dress that could have come out of any decade but this one. Her voice cracks as she talks, giving the impression that she's on the verge of tears. (Possibly a true impression: you start keeping track of the times she does burst into tears, and the count soon reaches thirteen.)

You have much leisure time to make these observations, for Louise talks nonstop. Forty-five minutes ago you asked a simple question, and she is still going strong. Listening to Louise is like moving the dial from one radio station to another, eavesdropping on talk shows that are all covering unrelated topics. The difference is that Louise, not you, controls the dial.

"Louise, tell me about yourself," was how you began forty-five minutes ago, and she started at birth, recounting her life in the rather odd lilt of an ancient Hebrew prophet. "I am like Gideon, the least of the house of Manasseh, called out of a cornfield, a cotton patch. . . ." The cotton patch lay in north Georgia, which is where Louise grew up. She changes topics a few times, but eventually circles back to her health complications in childhood.

"I had double pneumonia three times before I reached the age of six, and very often a black couple would come to relieve my parents' nursing duties. Our house had no racial prejudice, none whatever. One night my lung collapsed, and my eyes rolled back in my head, and no one thought I would make it through the night. A neighbor offered to dig my grave. But—I believe it was a miracle—I woke up in the middle of the night, started breathing, and announced I wanted corn bread and cabbage. I still remember what Mother said. She said, 'Louise, you're not your own. God saved you for a purpose. Seek it out.' "

The tears start flowing. The memory has triggered a deep emotional response in Louise. "Oh, the Lord's ways are so beautiful, incomprehensible, so past finding out."

> You feel moved and inspired, but still have only the vaguest idea of how Louise spends her time.

You use the segue to interject a second question: "Is that when you felt called to serve God?" Immediately you learn about Louise's unconventional approach to applying the Bible. "You know how Isaiah 40 says, 'Wait upon the Lord'? Well, I've taken that as my motto. I want to wait on the Lord like a waitress waiting on tables. I want to serve him every day." And suddenly she has leaped forward twenty years and is describing her student days in Atlanta.

In the 1940s, while working full-time and going to evening school three nights a week, Louise volunteered for mission work in the slums of Atlanta, black neighborhoods with colorful names like Buttermilk Basin and Cabbagetown. "I would hold Bible clubs for the children. Most of the houses were built on stilts or concrete blocks, and when it rained we would sweep aside the cobwebs and climb up underneath the houses to hold our meetings. It was there that God opened up to me the great face of missions—the heartache, the sadness, the need. But I knew I needed more training, so after I finished my college courses I enrolled in a Southern Baptist seminary."

You have been warned that Louise is something of a pack rat, and sure enough she reaches under a table and hauls out a huge cardboard box of yellowed newspapers. She has marked feature articles that graphically describe those postwar slums, and she reads these aloud. Once again the tears flow. "Listen to this. Three girls, ages seven, nine, and eleven. Their mother, a prostitute, ties them to her bed for men to molest. Can you imagine it? It was just a massive sea of suffering in those days. The rest of the world went on as if the people in those neighborhoods did not exist. They were like the thirteenth tribe of Israel, a lost tribe. This was the greatest slum south of Chicago."

Louise has a detailed inner map of the changing sociology of the city, but it bears little resemblance to what you might read in a sociology textbook. It goes like this: "In the 1950s, the inner city began to envelop the main churches. God was standing there saying to us, 'Don't run! Stay! I have brought the masses to you.' Like I once heard from a black preacher, God said to Moses at the edge of the Red Sea, 'Don't just do something—stand there!' And that's what God was telling the church, just to stand.

"But we didn't stand, most of us. We ran. And so in the 1960s rioters started burning those cities down. God wanted his people to lower the racial barriers, to overcome the differences, to open the doors. If we wouldn't do it on our own, others would do it for us.

"And then in the 1970s God said, 'The church hasn't met the challenge of the fifties and the sixties, so I'll move on with my Spirit in my own way.' That's when the Jesus movement broke out [among young people], and there came a new outpouring of God's Spirit. God was so far ahead of us that many people never have caught up."

During those decades, Louise tried not to get left in the dust. She had found a husband in seminary, and he took the pastorate at a large inner-city church, all white, in what Atlantans like to call a "changing neighborhood." The neighborhood was changing far too fast for most white tastes, and the church was divided over whether to integrate racially. The issue of black membership finally came to a head at a fractious congregational meeting.

Louise remembers it well: "I was so proud of my husband and the stand he took. The church was packed. Conservatives had recruited scores of members still on the rolls who hadn't been to church in years. We voted by secret ballot, and by a margin of thirty-nine votes they decided to keep black people out. My husband resigned, and we lost everything—our income, the parsonage, everything. And you know something, I think the Spirit of God left the church that day. It started dying from that day on. Those were dark times, when we wondered if God had abandoned the city."

Four years later Louise's husband died. She stayed in the neighborhood, living on a modest income provided through the Southern Baptist Home Mission Board. In the 1970s, she mostly worked with children, teaching 1,500 a week in Bible classes. As she got to know the children, she got to know their needs. Soon she was distributing food and clothing, appearing at the Juvenile Court as a character witness, visiting hospitals and prisons. If Louise came across children from abusive families, she would ask their parents to let the children move in with her. In this way, she has been "mother" to some fourteen children. "Isn't God good! He knew exactly what he was doing by not giving me any children of my own. I would have been so burdened down I wouldn't be there for these precious little ones.

"I never planned a formal 'ministry.' My goodness! God would just bring these wonderful people into my life. The Baptist church allowed me to use their facilities on weekdays, as long as no blacks came on Sunday. One day I brought in a little black girl who had just accepted Jesus. She asked the pastor if she could be baptized, and the church went into a kind of panic. Within two months the congregation had moved to Stone Mountain, twenty miles east of Atlanta.

"But for some reason the Baptists kept sending me support, and soon a Presbyterian church opened its doors. They gave me their keys and said, 'Louise, you can bring anybody you want into our church—black, yellow, prostitute, alcoholic, anybody.' Isn't it marvelous how God provides? Remember that psalm about the pit and the miry clay? God's still rescuing people out of the pit, and it's too bad some of these churches didn't stick around and get to know them."

All this time, Louise had to file official reports with the Board of Home Missions. Her method of ministry did not fit any of their established categories. Louise calls her ministry a "Jericho Road ministry," after the parable of the Good Samaritan who helped a man left for dead on the road to Jericho. "I don't have a board or committees, or anything like that. I used to work through local churches, but they all kept moving away. I just work on my own. People give me food and clothing, and I distribute it around."

Louise gets a little testy when questioned about planning and organization. "How would anyone go about scheduling a Jericho Road ministry? You just walk down the road and look for victims, and it may be daylight before you ever reach Jericho. You can't structure people's crises. They hit with no warning, like a tornado. And I've been here so long, lots of these people call me before they call the police or fire department. We've made missions so difficult, don't you think? It's just a matter of living for God, and loving those around you. The Lord structures my every day. And at the end of every day I feel like falling on my knees to sing the Hallelujah Chorus."

The Presbyterian church finally closed down, too, after its congregation had shrunk to a few dozen members. They asked Louise to keep using the building, hoping that her presence might discourage vandalism. She practically moved into the rundown sanctuary, holding her Bible classes there, teaching unwed mothers, giving shelter to the homeless. Eventually, a few young professional Christians with a social conscience moved into the neighborhood, and the church revived. "You see," Louise says triumphantly, "God never left this place! He was here all along."

Y ou listen to stories from Louise all afternoon. As the sun starts to drop below the trees outside, you feel moved and inspired, but still you have only the vaguest picture of how Louise actually spends her time. What happened yesterday, for example, or today? Does she just wake up in the morning and wait for the phone to ring? You interrupt her and ask that question.

"Morning? No, no, it usually rings at night. Let's see—yesterday. Oh, yes. A mother I'd been working with called me around supper time. I went right over and found her sitting in the middle of the floor with bruises all over her face. Her husband had been beating her again. She had a big bottle of prescription medicine beside her on the floor, and she told me she'd been fighting all day not to take it. Two kids were crying their lungs out in the next room. I had brought some groceries with me, so we cooked a dinner, calmed the kids down, and spent two hours cleaning house together. By the end of that time we were both singing hymns as we worked.

"When I got home, the fatigue set in. I got another call about midnight. Three elderly people had been shut up in a house for three days without food. My first response was, 'Lord, I'm tired. I want to go to bed.' But Jesus said to love your neighbor as yourself, and if that was my mother in that apartment, I'd want someone to feed her. So I went to the store right quick. They lived on the third floor. Dragging those groceries up the first two flights, I felt bone-tired. But somewhere about the second-floor landing, it was like God hit me with a shot of B-12. I went in and spent three hours with those lovely ladies. We had a banquet in the middle of the night. I was so excited I could hardly fall asleep when I went home."

What about burnout? "Well, sure, I get tired, and when it gets too bad I head up to the farm in north Georgia for a week or so. But Jesus said to seek first the kingdom of God, and all these things will be added unto you. And you know something, that's true. Sometimes discouraging things happen. Last year my house was broken into three times. I usually know who did it—kids after money for drugs. Last time it was two kids I've tried to help for years. I tracked them down, told them that of course

I wouldn't press charges, and asked if I could pray with them. The best thing happened. I heard from the one boy's mother that her son told her, 'Miz Adamson, she bugs us. I break into her house, and she comes back with a load of food and a Bible. That bugs me.' Now isn't that great! If he'd gone to prison, he would come out so mad you could never reach him for Jesus. Now he can't get Jesus out of his mind!"

Louise is crying again, and when she stops, she tells another story, about one of her foster children. She currently serves as official guardian for twelve children assigned to her by the Juvenile Court. You listen to these stories until the sun disappears completely and the lights come on and it is time to go. On the street outside, after you have said good-bye to Louise and after she has prayed aloud for your safe journey home, you run into one of the fourteen children that Louise has raised.

The girl's name is Faye, and when you tell her you've spent the after-noon with Louise, she begins talking excitedly, just like Louise. "What a woman! Every day I pray, 'Lord, teach me to be more like Louise. Teach me to love people and not be so selfish.' I was eight years old when I moved in with Louise, and I had no idea what love was. We lived in a tenement with the lights and gas cut off and my dad in prison. When my little brother was burned all over in a fire we'd lit to keep warm, Louise offered to help out by raising me. For the first time in my life I was with someone who wasn't afraid to touch me and hug me. She told me that the most important thing in life was that Jesus loved me, and then she put arms to his love. She'd wake me up at three in the morning, say, 'Come on, honey, we've got to go.' I would sleep on a pallet on the floorboard of the car while she ran in to check on somebody else who had just got burned out of her home.

"I had a sister who stomped out of home thirteen years ago and said, 'I'm never coming back to this God-forsaken place. She was chasing wealth, and married a boy she thought would make her rich. It didn't work out. Her kids are right back here, strung out on dope. But I guess the thing I learned most from Louise was that God has not forsaken this place. Not by a long shot. He's still here."

FINDING GOD in Unexpected PLACES

* * *

Louise Adamson is a true eccentric. Her house blends in well in the neighborhood she serves. Old sofas clutter the front porch (waiting for placement with needy refugees). Rattletrap cars sit on the front lawn (soon to be donated to poor families). She doesn't fit the pattern of any minister or social worker you know. She has no staff or organized program. She doesn't give tax deductible receipts to her donors (although for years she has faithfully saved all her own receipts—in a large pasteboard box in her living room). If you asked her about a five-year plan, or even a five-day plan, she would stare at you blankly. She says she needs to stay free to listen to God's Spirit. She simply wakes up each day and asks God to use her.

Meanwhile, in university offices, sociologists analyze the cycle of dependency in the underclass. In seminaries, urban specialists devise strategies to address the problems of the inner city. Government task forces study the drug problem and the crisis of the homeless. These programs will soak up billions of dollars, and many years will pass before results begin to show.

It occurs to you, as you guide your car onto an expressway ramp that curves around the stadium, that if every Christian in Atlanta responded to the gospel like Louise, the city would be a very different place. You find yourself longing for more eccentrics.

CHAPTER 15

Dr. Donahue's Crack Solutions

For the first time ever I watched an entire episode of *Donahue* on TV, and it was a classic. The topic of the day, "crack babies," followed up sensational reports in the *New York Post* and *Wall Street Journal* on yet another social problem that should terrify the American public.

First, the *Post* reporters were brought out to explain the problem. Around four million babies have been born to users of "crack," an exceptionally potent form of cocaine. These babies, born addicted and underweight, often have severe physical and emotional problems. The oldest of these offspring are now invading the classrooms of public schools, which already have their hands full with "normal" children. Crack children have an impossibly low attention span, exhibit hostile behavior, and show few signs of a moral conscience.

In short, the U.S. is being overrun by a large group of young citizens who will further strain health and education resources, and who give every indication of eventually adding to the burdens of juvenile and adult detention centers. The reporters predicted that crack children would become the number one social problem in the U.S.

Donahue's producers had managed to persuade two crack mothers—one African American, one white—to appear on the show, and after the *Post* reporters outlined the scope of the problem Donahue introduced the two. Tension in the audience visibly increased. The middle-class, mostly female spectators, who had just heard that drug users were unleashing a plague on their society, now had a chance to face down in person two real-life carriers of that plague.

The white crack mother seemed on drugs at that very moment. Slumping down in her chair behind the protective shield of dark glasses, she gave slurred, sluggish responses to questions. The African American woman, currently pregnant with her second crack baby, proved quite articulate. "I've been clean for two days now," she said. "Somebody was nice to me and showed me some respect. They put me up in a hotel room for two nights and treated me like a person, and for the first time I wanted to change. I wanted to be better. And so I didn't have to use the crack." Loud applause.

Donahue jumped in with a homily. "See, these women need compassion," he said, holding out an open hand in their direction. "We've got to get off our 'hickory stick' morality. What good will it do to punish these women?" More applause.

Then he turned to the African American woman and asked a question that was undoubtedly lurking in the minds of most of the audience. "Now, help us out here. We're trying to understand. You had one crack baby already, right? And you saw the physical problems that child went through. Yet you got pregnant again. Why?"

She thought for a moment. "Well, all I can say is, accidents do happen," she said at last. With that, she lost her sympathetic audience. Some booed and hissed. Others shook their heads angrily. As taxpayers, they would be asked to contribute tens of billions of dollars to pay for the problems presented by crack babies. Accidents may happen—but four million accidents?

A social worker, the final member of the panel, quickly jumped in. "The only way these women can support their habit is by prostitution, turning twenty to thirty tricks a night. In their health condition, they normally don't menstruate, and often don't notice they are pregnant until four or five months into term, too late for a legal abortion."

Judging by the comments and questions that followed, however, the audience had used up its reservoir of compassion. "Why should I have to pay for their irresponsible behavior?" asked one woman, trembling with anger. "Shouldn't they be the ones to face the consequences? And it's not just themselves they're hurting—what about all those innocent babies!"

Another suggested sterilizing any woman who delivered a crack baby. Donahue seized on her suggestion: "And should we sterilize alcohol-abusing mothers? Tobacco-abusing mothers? Should we turn the police loose to knock on doors and sniff out any mothers unfit to bear children?"

> For the first time ever I watched an entire episode of *Donahue* on TV, and it was a classic.

The woman appeared confused, but stood by her original suggestion. Something must be done.

So what can be done? Education is the answer, said the *Post* reporters. Yes, education, echoed the social worker. The articulate crack mother nodded in agreement; the sluggish one simply nodded.

I happened to be watching the Donahue show in a friend's living room, sitting next to a doctor who worked in Chicago's Cook County Hospital emergency room. As Donahue's guests rallied around the suggestion of education as the fix-all, this doctor suddenly laughed aloud. "The addicts I treat educate me about their condition," he said. "They like to portray themselves as poor, ignorant victims, but I've found many of them can interpret the charts on blood count and other vital stats better than most health workers."

If education were the simple answer, would crack have made such inroads among the literate middle class? If education were the answer, wouldn't the pregnant woman on the panel have given up her habit after

Dr. Donahue's Crack Solution

she bore her first child—or at least used a fail-safe birth control method? If education alone were the answer, smokers and alcoholics would now be extinct in America.

Alcoholics Anonymous discovered long ago that the path toward cure involves more than a quick-fix solution based on increased knowledge. In fact, it involves a change that seems more theological than educational. Somehow the "victim" of addictive behavior must regain an underlying sense of human dignity and choice, a profound reawakening that usually requires much time, attention, and love.

AA members recite their creed at every meeting, a creed that renounces the notion that any of us are helpless, ignorant victims of overwhelming forces. I am a human being, morally responsible, and the choices I make affect not only me but also my family and society all around me. I will need help—from my friends and family, from fellow abusers, from a Higher Power—but at the outset I must own my capability of moral choice.

I have long been impressed by the unique way Alcoholics Anonymous combines seeming opposites: compassion that still insists on moral responsibility; community support that somehow fosters individual dignity; self-actualization that comes from dependence on a Higher Power. It is only natural that these concepts sound like Christian theology, since AA was founded by committed Christians. But such ideas are rather difficult to communicate to a whole society—let alone to get across on the Phil Donahue show.

CHAPTER 16

Health and the God Factor

W hen Dr. David Larson was training for a career in psychiatry, faculty advisers warned him, "You'll harm your patients if you try to combine your Christian faith with the practice of psychiatry. It's clinically impossible." Instructors insisted that religion usually harms a person's mental health.

Does research confirm that notion? Larson wondered. Or is it a myth passed around in academic circles? His curiosity led him on a quest he has followed for fifteen years. He spends much of his time poring over academic journals and obscure research reports, pondering "negative curvilinear variables" and other data, seeking clues into how religion affects mental and physical health.

Right away Larson noticed that most research studies ignored the subject of religion altogether. This seemed odd, since 90 percent of Americans believe in God, 40 percent attend religious services weekly, and a large minority claim religion is "very important" in their lives. Could the omission reflect the antireligious bias of the field? Less than half of psychiatrists and psychologists claim to believe in God, and one survey found that 40 percent regard organized religion as "always, or usually, psychologically harmful."

Even though modern surveys tended to avoid explicit questions on faith, Larson found that some had asked basic questions about religious involvement. He examined these findings, then broadened his search to include anything that might indicate the effect of Christian commitment on health. What he found shocked him. A sampling:

- Regular church attenders live longer. Religiousness markedly reduces the incidence of heart attack, arteriosclerosis, and high blood pressure.

- Religious people are less likely to abuse alcohol, and far less likely to use illicit drugs. Conversely, one study found that 89 percent of alcoholics had lost interest in religion during their teenage years.

- Prison inmates who make a religious commitment are less likely than their counterparts to return to jail after release.

- Marital satisfaction and overall well-being tend to increase with church attendance; depression rates decline.

- Religious commitment offers some protection against one of the nation's greatest health problems: divorce. People who attend church regularly are more than twice as likely to remain married.

Protection against divorce is important for the following reasons:

- Divorce dramatically increases the likelihood of early death from strokes, hypertension, respiratory cancer, and intestinal cancer. Astonishingly, being divorced and a nonsmoker is only slightly less dangerous than smoking a pack or more a day and staying married! (Should divorce summons papers come with a Surgeon General's warning, too?)

- Divorce also disrupts mental health, especially for men. The suicide rate for white males goes up by a factor of four with divorce, and they have ten times the probability of needing psychiatric care.

- Divorce takes a devastating toll on children. Proportionately twice as many criminals come from single-parent homes. Indeed, family structure proves more effective than economic status in predicting a life in crime. Children from broken homes are more likely to do poorly in school, abuse drugs, and attempt suicide.

In short, Larson found that religious commitment, far from causing health problems, has a pronounced effect on reducing them. "In essence the studies empirically verify the wisdom of the book of Proverbs," he says. "Those who follow biblical values live longer, enjoy life more, and are less diseased. The facts are in; we need to get the word out." As a consultant to the National Institute of Mental Health and a fellow of the newly formed Paul Tournier Institute (sponsored by the Christian Medical and Dental Society), he seeks to do just that.

> Why does Nevada have so many heart attacks while Utah has so few?

W hen I met David Larson, I was in the process of coauthoring a book with Dr. Paul Brand, then president of the International Christian Medical and Dental Society. He told me of a conference he had attended in Arizona in which representatives from the Public Health Service, including the Centers for Disease Control and the Food and Drug Administration, met together to discuss health trends and to set priorities for new programs. During the conference, he kept a running list of all the behavior-related problems on the agenda and the time devoted to each: heart disease and hypertension exacerbated by stress, AIDS, sexually transmitted diseases, emphysema and lung cancer caused by cigarette smoking, fetal damage stemming from maternal alcohol and drug abuse, diabetes and other diet-related disorders, violent crime, automobile accidents involving alcohol. These were the endemic, even epidemic concerns for health experts in the United States.

It occurred to Brand that a comparable gathering of experts in India, where he had worked for many years, would have dealt instead with malaria, polio, dysentery, tuberculosis, typhoid, and leprosy. After valiantly conquering most of those infectious diseases, the U.S. has now substituted new health problems for old, many of which stem from lifestyle choices.

The Public Health Service conference was taking place in Scottsdale, Arizona. That state's neighbor to the west, Nevada, ranks near the high end on most mortality tables, while its northern neighbor, Utah, ranks near the bottom. Both states are relatively wealthy and their citizens well educated, and they share a similar climate. The difference, studies suggest, is probably explained by lifestyle factors. Utah is the seat of Mormonism, which frowns on alcohol and tobacco. Family ties remain strong in Utah and marriages tend to endure. Nevada, in contrast, has twice the incidence of divorce and a far higher rate of alcohol and tobacco consumption, not to mention the unique stress associated with gambling.

Dr. David Larson, who lives near Washington, D.C., believes such facts should influence public policy. "Decision makers can't be expected to write laws that reflect biblical values," he admits. "But I've found they do respond to two things: 1. staying alive and 2. saving money. We know beyond doubt that divorce, for example, hurts all parties and costs society dearly; shouldn't public policy somehow favor stable marriages?"

Larson points out that the key factor is the degree of religious commitment, not any particular affiliation. Dedicated Mormons, Jews, Catholics, and Protestants all manifest improved health. The psychoanalyst Carl Jung wrote:

I have treated many hundreds of patients, the larger number being Protestants, a smaller number Jews and not more than five or six believing Catholics. Among all my patients in the second half of my life . . . there has not been one whose problem in the last resort was not that of finding a religious outlook on life. It is safe to say that every one of them fell ill because he lost that which the living religions of every age have given their followers and none of them has really been healed who did not regain his religious outlook.

According to Larson, it would be difficult to concoct a better recipe for health than Paul's nine-word prescription given in Galatians 5: love, joy, peace, patience, kindness, goodness, faithfulness, gentleness, and self-control. Paul playfully comments, "Against such things there is no law." In view of Larson's findings, perhaps we should add a footnote, "To promote such things there should be a law."

I have my doubts whether any amount of empirical data will persuade the U.S. Congress to enact legislation along the lines Larson's research suggests. As a nation, we seem far more interested in preserving the right to destroy ourselves. However, the findings do hint at an approach that may prove useful to the church in the twenty-first century.

In the not-so-distant past the American church and state recognized many of the same values: sacredness and dignity of human life, sexual fidelity, family stability, discipline, moderation. Increasingly, those values have been drifting apart, and the church may not be able to stop that trend in a secularized society. But we can strive to fulfill Jesus' original challenge: to serve as the salt of the earth, the light of the world, a city on a hill.

Although we may not convert the whole hill, we need not be ashamed of erecting a different kind of city on the landscape of our troubled planet. As the research clearly shows, what is "good" in the moral sense, in the city of God, is also good in the pragmatic sense, in the city of man. To paraphrase philosopher John Locke, Christianity makes sense in this world as well as in the next.

CHAPTER 17

Shakespeare and the Politicians

I n a moment of idealism, I made a New Year's resolution to read all thirty-eight of Shakespeare's plays in one year. So much for idealism: three years have passed and I still have seven plays to go. Yet, to my surprise, fulfilling the task has seemed far more like entertainment than like work. I always look forward to the designated Shakespeare evening. I have found the plays to be unfailingly witty and profound, and oddly up to date.

Once, with CNN playing softly in the background, I decided to reflect on what I had learned. "Love cools, friendship falls off, brothers divide; in cities, mutinies, in countries, discord; in palaces, treason; and the bond cracked twixt son and father." Those words from *King Lear* sounded suspiciously like commentators describing the modern world. Too bleak for most generations' taste, *King Lear* was performed for centuries in a happy-ending version. Now that modern sensibilities have caught up with its dark vision, it has become Shakespeare's most revered play.

"Each new morn new widows howl, new orphans cry, new sorrows strike heaven on the face"—was that *Macbeth* or Jesse Jackson? Shakespeare's depictions of crime, injustice, war, treachery, and greed demonstrate that, no matter what either political party says, these problems are not mutations in America of the 1990s; they have been around since Eden.

Some major differences between the Elizabethan view of the world and our own stood out as well. Listening to politicians from both parties, I get the distinct notion that if we could just keep the economy rolling and clean up the drug problem and educate all those misguided kids in gangs, why then a golden age would return to America. Social problems (the closest modern equivalent to "evil") trace back to poverty and lack of education.

Shakespeare would disagree. "They are as sick that surfeit with too much as they that starve with nothing," observed the maid of an heiress in *The Merchant of Venice*. Shakespeare showed genuine respect for the decency of the lower classes. The real villains were rich and powerful, people like Macbeth and Richard III who had every advantage of education, wealth, and fine breeding. I am struck that many greats in literature—Shakespeare, Tolstoy, Balzac, Dickens—scoff at the idea that poverty lies at the root of evil. For them, evil raises its ugly head most monstrously within the upper classes.

King Lear states it best: "Through tattered clothes small vices do appear; robes and furred gowns hide all. Plate sin with gold." Lear learned this lesson the hard way. Cast out of his own castle by his avaricious daughters, he wandered alone through a terrific rainstorm, finally taking shelter in a cave with a refugee. The experience revealed to him a "theology of reversal" and for the first time he understood the plight of the poor and homeless:

> Poor naked wretches, wheresoe'r you are,
> That bide the pelting of this pitiless storm,
> How shall your houseless heads and unfed sides,
> Your looped and windowed raggedness, defend you
> From seasons such as these? O, I have ta'en
> Too little care of this! Take physic, pomp;
> Expose thyself to feel what wretches feel,
> That thou mayst shake the superflux to them
> And show the heavens more just.

It is not the only scene in Lear that rings with overtones of the Incarnation of Christ.

Republicans blame a Democratic administration for society's ills while Democrats blame a Republican Congress—or vice versa, depending on the decade. Shakespeare's characters are as likely to implicate God. "Wilt thou, O God, fly from such gentle lambs and throw them in the entrails of the wolf? When didst thou sleep when such a deed was done?" cries one after a murderous crime. "O God, seest thou this, and bearest so long?" laments another.

> I find it wonderfully refreshing to read of people who have a sense of personal *destiny* about them.

These anguished cries ironically reveal a belief in Providence that underlies all of Shakespeare's plays. You only rail against God if you still believe God is active. As seen most clearly in the multiplay cycle centering on Henry VI, for Shakespeare history involved more than the rise and fall of rulers and nations. The turmoil and civil strife in England signified God's judgment. This is a harsh message, one I never hear on CNN.

In Shakespeare's time, people still lived out their days under the shadow of divine reward and punishment, an assumption that tends to put boundaries around evil. In *Richard III*, a hired assassin trembles before his assignment, fearing "Not to kill him, having a warrant, but to be damned for killing him, from the which no warrant can defend me." And in *Henry VI* the Earl of Warwick prays, ". . . ere my knee rise from the earth's cold face, I throw my hands, mine eyes, my heart to Thee, Thou setter-up and plucker-down of kings." Our leaders could use a dose of such humility.

One last irony struck me as I pondered the Elizabethan era and our own. Comparing Shakespeare's characters with modern-day politicians,

I could not help thinking how we as men and women have shrunk. The "politics of marginalization" rules in the U.S.A. Rioters riot because they can't help it, teens get pregnant because their drives overpower them, "pro-choice" women choose abortion because they "have no choice." The message is clear: We are products of our genes, our families, and our cultures, nothing more.

In contrast, the characters in Shakespeare stride like giants across the stage. I find it wonderfully refreshing to read of people who have a sense of personal *destiny* about them. These are not automatons or victims, but free individuals making choices, some malignant and some noble. As the master playwright insists, they must then live with the consequences. Lady Macbeth hoped otherwise: "A little water clears us of this deed," she said as she and her husband rinsed their hands of blood. How wrong she was.

Lady Macbeth died haunted by guilt, and her husband mourned her with these eloquent words of despair:

> Life's but a walking shadow, a poor player
> That struts and frets his hour upon the stage
> And then is heard no more. It is a tale
> Told by an idiot, full of sound and fury,
> Signifying nothing.

Shakespeare's plays alone offer enough evidence to refute that nihilism. As the Victorian scholar A. C. Bradley wrote, in words that apply to almost all of Shakespeare's characters, "No one ever closes a tragedy with the feeling that man is a poor mean creature. He may be wretched and he may be awful but he is not small." It's enough to make you nostalgic.

Why Do Muslims Hate Us?

For more than a decade Americans have watched on television as mobs of screaming Muslims, calling for "death to the Great Satan," burn our presidents in effigy. The geography of protest changes—first Iran and Libya, then Lebanon, then on to such places as Iraq and Algeria—but the zealousness does not. Some religious fanatics out there genuinely despise us.

Most Americans do not know what to make of these scenes. We fancy ourselves as friendly folks, quick to smile and lend a helping hand. Our political leaders seem to us more like congenial uncles than tyrants. The label "Great Satan" especially rankles, for we think of the U.S. as a Christian nation, far more devout than, say, Western Europe. At least we still go to church. How can anyone imagine us as nefarious or pagan?

Many historians foresee a great divide opening up again between the world's two largest religions, Christianity and Islam. In recent times we grew so used to the polarity of Communism versus capitalism that we forgot the Western world was once obsessed with a polarity of religion. It behooves us to understand each other, lest we stumble into another eight-hundred-year conflict.

Most Islamic criticisms of the West seem to revolve around the fusty word *materialism.* When that word describes the pursuit of wealth and consumer comforts, few Arab nations disapprove: thanks to oil revenues, the Persian Gulf is the wealthiest region in the world. But materialism also refs to a philosophical approach, a belief that human life consists mainly (or solely) in what takes place here and now, in the world of matter.

The disciples of Islam tend to view us as being obsessively concerned with this life, not the eternity to come. One reason Saddam Hussein gambled on an invasion of Kuwait was that he doubted the West, and the U.S. in particular, had the will to sacrifice thousands of lives. In contrast, the war between Iran and Iraq had already proved that hundreds of thousands of faithful Muslims would gladly die in "glorious martyrdom" if promised instant passage into paradise.

In one of the great ironies of history, Islam has co-opted the word *martyr*. Early Christians prevailed over Rome because they opted for eternal rewards instead of mere physical survival. The blood of the martyrs was the seed of the church. Nowadays you hear very little talk in the West about eternal rewards and much talk about techniques to keep death at bay. Young Arabs who study here come away impressed with, and often scandalized by, how much energy we invest in the physical life. Scout the magazine racks at a local drug store sometime, counting the titles devoted to body-building, diet, fashion, and naked women—all emblems of the prominence we give to materiality.

Puritanical is another Christian word co-opted by Islamic societies. During the Persian Gulf War, for the first time in recent memory U.S. soldiers had to get by without alcohol and *Playboy*, in deference to the strict Islamic code in Saudi Arabia. Few of them realized that the difference in moral standards between Islam and the West is philosophical, not just cultural.

In determining morality, American society tends to apply the bottom-line principle, "Does it hurt anyone else?" Thus pornography is legal, but not if it involves explicit violence or child molestation. You can get legally drunk as long as you do not break a neighbor's window or drive a car, endangering others. Violence on television is OK, because everyone knows the characters are just acting.

This yardstick of morality betrays our implicit materialism.

Whereas we define *hurt* in the most physical terms, Islamic societies see it in more spiritual terms. In that deeper sense, what could be more harmful than divorce, say, or pornography, or violence-as-entertainment, or even the cynical depiction of banal evil in a television show such as *Melrose Place?* It is from this vantage point that the U.S. has gained its reputation as "the Great Satan."

The same materialism shows through in our preferred methods of punishment. Americans are scandalized by such Islamic "brutalities" as beheadings, public beatings, and the amputation of thieves' hands. How could they be so cruel? we wonder. But we lock teenagers in cells crowded with abusive criminals; do we ever ponder what happens to their souls? "Do not be afraid of those who kill the body but cannot kill the soul," Jesus cautioned. And again, "It is better for you to lose one part of your body than for your whole body to go into hell."

We "infidels" have some lessons to learn.

T he Italian writer Umberto Eco *(The Name of the Rose, Foucault's Pendulum)* wrote a fascinating account of a trip across America titled *Travels in Hyperreality.* He, too, came away impressed with our basic materialism. Americans even give physical substance to their myths, he observed. Ancient Greeks celebrated their heroes in song and poetry around a campfire; Americans shake hands with them in fuzzy suits at Disneyland.

Religious television intrigued Eco: "If you follow the Sunday morning religious programs on TV you come to understand that God can be experienced only as nature, flesh, energy, tangible image. And since no preacher dares show us God in the form of a bearded dummy, or as a

Disneyland robot, God can only be found in the form of natural force, joy, healing, youth, health, economic increment." Where is the *mysterium tremendum,* Eco wondered; where is the holy, numinous, ineffable God?

I must confess that of the major world religions, Islam is hardest for me to understand and appreciate. I find its doctrine unconvincing and its fanatical fringe terrifying. Yet questions raised by Islam should trouble us Christians in the West. Islam has, above all, cherished the belief in a holy, numinous God. It has also nourished a profound allegiance to a spiritual and immortal life, not just a material and mortal one. We "infidels" have some lessons to learn.

CHAPTER 19

Those Were the Days, My Friend

Things fall apart; the centre cannot hold;
Mere anarchy is loosed upon the world,
The blood-dimmed tide is loosed, and everywhere
The ceremony of innocence is drowned;
The best lack all conviction, while the worst
Are full of passionate intensity.

—W. B. YEATS

J ust as the Depression and World War II marked an entire generation, the decade of the 1960s left its mark on their offspring. Those
of us who grew up in that tumultuous decade are still dealing with
its impact—all of society, in fact, is dealing with it.

I was ten when the sixties began, and twenty when it ended. In some
ways I passed through the decade protected by a Teflon™ shield of religion and subculture. I had never developed a taste for music written after 1890, and mind-altering drugs never tempted me. More, I spent the
later sixties on the campus of a Christian college: While secular university
students were holding college presidents hostage and bombing buildings,
our most daring protestors lobbied meekly against compulsory chapel.
Still, despite my isolation, I was profoundly affected by those years of dis-
content.

At the time, it appeared the world stood at a threshold. When

Parisian students took to the barricades in 1968, political conservatives shrieked about the end of all civilization and the unstoppable juggernaut of Communism. Christian gurus like Francis Schaeffer predicted mounting unrest that would lead to cultural anarchy. No one, absolutely no one, foretold what actually did take place over the next two decades: a withdrawal from political to personal concerns, a surge in M.B.A. degrees, the conquests of Yuppiedom, a retreat from civil rights activism, the election and reelection of Ronald Reagan, the phenomena of Rush Limbaugh and Newt Gingrich, the collapse of European Communism.

It became evident that the sixties represented, more than anything, a fluke of demographics. Baby Boomers were one of the few generations in U.S. history larger than the generation to follow them; naturally, their rite of passage would have a disproportionate impact. The population bulge moved through adolescence and young adulthood like a small pig moving through a boa constrictor: it surely changed the shape of its surroundings, but eventually, like everything else, it, too, was absorbed.

The sixties began with an emphasis on ideals: peace, love, community, justice, equality. A renewed emphasis on spirituality drove many high school and college students to "get high on Jesus." A passion for ideals, though, is always difficult to sustain, and gradually the focus shifted from *substance* toward *style*. American corporations jumped in, cranking out designer blue jeans and sneakers, machine-cut leather fringe, and prewashed, tie-dyed T-shirts. Facial hair sprouted in unlikely places: on bankers and politicians and stockbrokers. Music groups like the Grateful Dead, who had begun as anti-establishment rebels, became billion-dollar properties.

As the ideals faded, or got co-opted, what remained was an emphasis on physicality. Consider what has endured as a legacy from the sixties: an active involvement with the outdoors; music that can be felt, literally, in the body's vibrating cells; a body-consciousness expressed through meditation, t'ai chi, or other New Age transmutations; drugs;

and, of course, the sexual revolution. All these features of our modern landscape express a heightened physicality that traces back to the sixties.

I find it ironic, and sad, that so many of the lofty ideals from the sixties have evaporated, leaving us with mere physical emblems, for what marked me during the sixties had nothing to do with these emblems. I think back with nostalgia on the passion of that decade. Though wild and unformed, that passion was strong enough to prompt thousands of clergy and students to head south on buses and risk their lives for a cause in Mississippi and Alabama, and strong enough to inspire students to resist a war they could not support. In the sixties, people thought with their hearts more than with their heads.

> The odd thing is, many important questions raised in the sixties are now more relevant than ever.

> *since feeling is first*
> *who pays any attention*
> *to the syntax of things?*
>
> —E E CUMMINGS

The sixties made us question cherished national values like global power, unlimited economic growth, and conspicuous consumption. If someone inquired about career goals, you would never hear the answer, "I think I'll specialize in arbitrage, or maybe junk bond financing." The respectable response then was "social work" or "legal services for the poor." Students questioned everyday things, too, like the macho ritual of football, and lusty beauty pageants.

Today, beauty pageants, football, and economic growth are all thriving. Apparently, the boa constrictor has absorbed the lump. The odd thing is, many important questions raised in the sixties are now more relevant than ever. People worried about the environment back then, long before anyone had heard such phrases as "greenhouse effect" and "ozone depletion." They worried about the national debt LBJ was piling up to pay for the war in Vietnam; those amounts would barely cover a month's interest on the national debt of the nineties. They worried about overpopulation at a time when the brittle earth supported two billion *fewer* human beings. Maybe the main problem with the spirit of the sixties is that it surfaced thirty years too soon.

I have a vague premonition that we haven't seen the end of convulsive protest. Perhaps the youth of the next century will resume marching in the streets, in protest against secularism, the monstrous national debt we've bequeathed them, and the polluted, overcrowded, soil-depleted, clearcut, strip-mined planet we've left behind. And, who knows, we oldsters who grew up during the sixties may take to the streets again as well. I have a hunch that if we do so, next time around we will be agitating for increased social security benefits, health care, and other legislative largesse we've come to call "entitlements."

CHAPTER 20

Running Away from Fugitives

I just have the feeling the country's headed in the wrong direction," said one friend of mine. Many people share her uneasiness. Violent crime has increased 560 percent since the 1960s. Promiscuity—in sex, in drugs, in violence, in consumption—has become the spirit of the age. The United States can be considered a Christian nation only in the loosest sense of the term. "God will turn his back on America," said my friend, shaking her head sadly.

All this concern about "the decline of America" got me wondering how much attention God pays to national boundaries. Does God really judge the United States or any other country *as a national entity?*

Certainly the Old Testament shows God dealing with national entities: the prophets called down judgment on Israel and Judah, as well as Philistia, Assyria, and Babylon. But the New Testament seems to introduce a major shift: God is now working not primarily through nations, but through an invisible kingdom that transcends nations. Jesus stressed "the kingdom of heaven" as the central focus of God's activity on earth, a kingdom that permeates society so as to gradually affect the whole, like salt sprinkled on meat.

As I now reflect on Jesus' stories of the kingdom, I sense that much uneasiness among Christians today stems from a confusion of the two kingdoms, visible and invisible. Each time an election rolls around, Christians debate whether this or that candidate is "God's man" for the White

House. Projecting myself back into Jesus' time, I have difficulty imagining him pondering whether Tiberius, Octavius, or Julius Caesar was "God's man" for the empire. What took place in Rome was on another plane entirely from the kingdom of God.

The apostle Paul cared deeply about individual churches in Galatia, Ephesus, Corinth, and Rome, but I find no indication that he gave any thought to a "Christianized" Roman Empire. The Revelation of John continues the pattern: that book records specific messages to seven churches but dismisses the political entity of Rome as "Babylon the great the mother of prostitutes and of the abominations of the earth."

Some historians argue that the church loses sight of its original mission as it moves closer to the seat of power. Witness the era of Constantine, and the Dark Ages, and Europe just before the Reformation. We may be seeing history repeat itself. The church has faced the constant temptation of becoming the "morals police" of society.

In 1991, as Communism fell in Poland, 70 percent of Poles approved of the Catholic church as a moral and spiritual force. Now only 40 percent approve, mainly because of its "interference" in politics. Modern Poland does not practice church-state separation: a new media law says radio and TV broadcasts must "respect the Christian system of values," and the state funds the teaching of Catholicism in Polish public schools. Yet the new coziness between church and government has resulted in a loss of respect for the church.

At various points in U.S. history (the 1850s, the time of Prohibition, and most recently the Moral Majority movement of the 1980s), the Christian church has marked an ascendancy into politics. Now, it appears, the church and politics may be heading in different directions. The more I understand Jesus' message of the kingdom of God, the less alarm I feel over that trend. Our real challenge, the focus of our energy, should not be to Christianize the United States (always a losing battle) but rather to strive to be Christ's church in an increasingly hostile world. As Karl

Barth said, "[The church] exists . . . to set up in the world a new sign which is radically dissimilar to [the world's] own manner and which contradicts it in a way which is full of promise."

Ironically, if indeed the United States is sliding down a slippery moral slope, that may better allow the church to set up "a new sign . . . which is full of promise." Already I see some evidence of that trend. Magazine writers, sociologists, and hostile politicians have all had to conclude that "Dan Quayle Was Right" about the grievously harmful effects of single-parent families. Meanwhile, sociologist Robert Bellah, after interviewing hundreds of married couples, identified evangelical Christians as the only group who could articulate a reason for marriage commitments that went beyond selfish interests. Research such as that uncovered by Dr. David Larson increasingly supports the healthy side-benefits of a life of faith.

> All the concern about "the decline of America" got me wondering how much attention God pays to national boundaries.

"In a world of fugitives," said T. S. Eliot, "the person taking the opposite direction will appear to run away." As America slides, I will work and pray for the kingdom of God to advance. If the gates of hell cannot prevail against the church, the contemporary political scene hardly offers much threat.

CHAPTER 21

Dispatch from the Culture Wars

B ecause cartoons reveal a lot about the general drift of culture, I have been collecting a few around a common theme:

• The *New Yorker* magazine pictured a waiter in an expensive restaurant explaining the menu to a patron: "The ones with asterisks are those recommended by the religious right."

• A nationally syndicated political cartoonist drew a church building with a "Christian Coalition" sign on the front. From inside comes the voice, "Reverend Falwell, Reverend Robertson, there's a gentleman waiting outside to see you. He says he's not a Republican." Their reply: "Tell him to get lost!" Outside the church stands Jesus.

• Yet another political cartoon depicted a classic American church building with the sign out front, "First Church of Anti-Clinton."

The culture wars have been heating up on both sides. Even as Christians feel like an embattled minority with their values under constant attack, the surrounding secular culture sees Christians as a growing threat.

I fully support the right, and indeed the responsibility, of Christians to get involved in politics. In moral crusades such as abolition, civil rights, and anti-abortion, Christians have led the way. I do worry, though, about an increasing tendency to see the labels "evangelical Christian" and "Religious Right" as interchangeable. The gospel of Jesus was not primarily a political platform.

People in Jesus' time who looked to him as their political savior were constantly befuddled by his choice of companions. He became known as a friend of tax collectors, a group clearly identified with the foreign exploiters. Though he denounced the religious system of his day, he treated a leader like Nicodemus with respect, and though he spoke against the dangers of money and of violence, he showed love and compassion toward a rich young ruler and a Roman centurion.

In short, Jesus honored the dignity of each person whether he agreed with him or her or not. Anyone, even a half-breed with five husbands or a thief nailed to a cross, was welcome to join his kingdom. The person was more important than any category or label.

I feel convicted by this quality of Jesus every time I get involved in a cause I strongly believe in. How easy it is to join the politics of polarization, to find myself shouting across the picket lines at the "enemy" on the other side. How hard it is to remember that the kingdom of God calls me to love the woman who has just emerged from the abortion clinic (and, yes, even her doctor), the promiscuous person who is dying of AIDS, the wealthy landowner who is exploiting God's creation. If I cannot show love to such people, then I need to ask if I have understood Jesus' gospel.

A political movement by nature draws lines, makes distinctions, pronounces judgment; in contrast, Jesus' love cuts across lines, transcends distinctions, and dispenses grace. If my activism drives out such love, I betray his kingdom.

Not long ago, I attended a play based on stories from a support group comprising people with AIDS. The theater director said he decided to stage the play after hearing a local minister state that he celebrated each time he read an obituary of a young single man, believing each death to be yet another sign of God's disapproval. Increasingly, I fear, the church is viewed as an enemy of sinners.

How does one hold to high standards of moral purity while at the same time showing grace to those who fail those standards? Christian history offers few facsimiles of the pattern Jesus laid down. We give lip service to "hate the sin while loving the sinner," but how well do we practice this principle? All too often, sinners feel unloved by a church that, in turn, keeps altering its definition of sin—precisely the opposite of Jesus' pattern.

> How easy it is
> to shout across the
> picket lines at the
> "enemy" on the
> other side.

The early church began well, placing a high premium on moral purity. Baptismal candidates had to undergo long periods of instruction, and church discipline was rigorously enforced. Yet even pagan observers were attracted to the way Christians cared for each other and devoted themselves to the sick and the poor.

A major change took place with the emperor Constantine, who first legalized Christianity and made it a state-subsidized religion. At the time, his reign appeared to be the faith's greatest triumph: the emperor was now using state funds to build churches and sponsor theological conferences rather than to persecute Christians for not worshiping him. Sadly, the triumph did not come without cost. The state began appointing bishops and other church offices, and a hierarchy grew up that neatly replicated the hierarchy of the empire itself. Christian bishops soon began imposing morality on society at large.

I realize, as I reflect on the life of Jesus, how far we have come from the divine balance he set out for us. Listening to the sermons and reading the writings of the contemporary church in the U.S., I some-times detect more of Constantine than of Jesus. The man from Nazareth was a sinless friend of sinners, a pattern that should convict us on both counts.

CHAPTER 22

A Whiff of Something Lethal

Novelist Walker Percy died in May 1990, two weeks shy of his seventy-fourth birthday. On that day Christian writers of fiction or nonfiction (I hate that word, defining a craft by what it is *not*) felt a sense of loss. Percy was one of the great guiding lights of faith, a writer skilled enough to capture the ear of a world that little values it.

Percy was forty-five years old when he published his first novel, *The Moviegoer*. He had trained as a medical doctor, with a particular interest in psychiatry, but during his residency he contracted tuberculosis, probably as a result of performing autopsies on derelicts. The year was 1941, and as Percy's friends were enlisting for the war in Europe, he was confined to a sanitarium in Lake Saranac, New York. For weeks on end he would see no one but the aides who brought him meals, a few fellow patients, and an occasional doctor.

Percy used his five years of recuperation to read and to reflect on the state of the world. How was it that Germany, the epitome of advanced Western civilization, was suddenly acting like a barbarian tribe? Percy read philosophy, especially the modern existentialists, but found the sanest explanations in Søren Kierkegaard, the melancholy Dane who had first protested against German rationalism.

Kierkegaard had said, "Hegel told everything about the world except one thing: what it is to be a man and to live and die." Percy began to realize that, in his words, "as a scientist I knew so very much about man, but had little idea what man is." He sensed that while the scientific method had superbly analyzed humanity as *organisms* in an environment, in the process it had lost sight of us as *selves* in a world. Modern human beings had progressed in every way but the most important way: morally, spiritually.

Nietzsche and then Hitler had simply taken the scientific method to its logical conclusion: If humanity merely represents another gene pool, how can we claim such unique properties as reason, freedom, "inalienable rights," and human dignity? What allows us to grant intrinsic worth to any one individual if there are indeed no transcendental values? Percy sensed the modern dilemma that Dostoevsky had expressed years before: "Without God, anything is permitted."

The war ended, the good guys won, and America settled into the comfortable suburban consumerism of the Eisenhower era. Walker Percy married, converted to Catholicism, and began to raise a family. Yet still he fretted over the basic question, "What is a human being?" He never did get around to practicing medicine.

Over the next decade, Percy wrote rather dense philosophical essays for such journals as *Thought, Philosophy and Phenomenological Research,* and *Partisan Review.* All of them circled around the question of meaning. Percy saw in the beat generation and in early hippies symptoms of the alienation of modern humanity. Nothing appeared on the horizon to replace the Christian notion of man as a creature endowed with the image of God, but fallen and in need of redemption.

The essays make fascinating reading, and many have been collected in *The Message in the Bottle.* But soon Percy searched for a way to express his ideas on spiritual homelessness to a wider audience. That's when he turned to fiction.

The Moviegoer, written for a $300 advance, attracted a few favorable reviews but scant attention until it was awarded the National Book Award for 1961, beating out Joseph Heller's *Catch-22* and J. D. Salinger's *Franny and Zooey.* Suddenly the literati had to take note of this "failed doctor" (Percy's term) who had the audacity to write a novel of ideas in an age of deconstructionism, this southerner who dared break the mold of southern novelists by writing about country clubs, not cotton fields.

Percy wrote slowly, producing a total of six novels over twenty-six years. *Lancelot,* though in a thoroughly modern setting, gives oblique homage to the legend of King Arthur. *Love in the Ruins* and *The Thanatos Syndrome* tell the story of Dr. Tom More (another homage to England); and *The Last Gentleman* and *The Second Coming* share the main character Will Barrett. Some

> Something is wrong with society, Walker Percy said, and one of the novelist's tasks is to isolate the bacillus and give the sickness a name.

have termed the novels apocalyptic, and indeed the titles themselves betray a hint of decline and doom. *Malaise* is a more accurate characterization, for Percy's protagonist is typically a troubled, rootless wanderer. Like reading a diagnostic chart on a century, reading these novels takes study, some skill. Percy had quoted Kierkegaard in *The Moviegoer:* "The specific character of despair is precisely this: It is unaware of being despair."

Autobiographical elements turn up, especially in the Will Barrett stories. Percy grew up in Birmingham, Alabama, in a new home on the edge of a golf course, a setting not unlike Barrett's. More poignantly, Barrett is haunted by his father's suicide; Percy was eleven when his own father killed himself.

It would be a travesty to view Percy's fiction as a form of propaganda, an Ayn Rand–like device to communicate personal philosophy. Judged by rigorous literary standards, the novels earned for him a place in the front rank of American writers. On the other hand, Percy himself described his fiction as diagnostic. Something is wrong with society, he said, and one of the novelist's tasks is to isolate the bacillus and give the sickness a name.

Percy risked his literary reputation by continuing to crank out essays detailing his diagnosis. In the breezy and funny *Lost in the Cosmos*, he took on scientism, soap operas, genetic manipulation, Phil Donahue, and pornography. The title captures one of Percy's favorite themes: that humankind is an orphan lost in the cosmos. The book playfully promises to reveal, among other things, "how you can survive in the Cosmos about which you know more and more while knowing less and less about yourself, this despite 10,000 self-help books, 100,000 psychotherapists, and 100 million fundamentalist Christians." Modern man resembles a castaway on a desert island who tries to interpret the message in a bottle washed ashore—or a prisoner in an isolation cell straining to hear a code tapped out on the wall. Percy believed he had heard those messages, and they were the echoes of orthodox Christianity.

Percy saw grave danger in a modern world that has made technocrats and scientists lords and sovereigns. We are told that human problems are being solved, but signs of despair and alienation in the young, in the wealthy suburbanites, in the Swedish bourgeois, prove otherwise. In such a world, the artist must function like a canary lowered into the mine shaft to test the air. Walker Percy had caught a whiff of something lethal.

Although trained as a scientist, Percy nevertheless viewed with suspicion the promise of modern technology. His diagnosis reads like a blend of George Orwell and Jacques Ellul. Utopian experiments of Nazism and Communism had both proposed a new society, a new form of human being. Aiming for "angelism," though, they ended up instead with "bestialism." Selfish American materialism, Percy believed, may be more subtle but is no less dangerous. It, too, leaves unanswered the most basic questions of meaning. "If the first great intellectual discovery of my life was the beauty of the scientific method, surely the second was the discovery of the singular predicament of man in the very world which has been transformed by this science," he concluded.

* * *

Percy was well aware of the challenge he faced in presenting an alternative: "The Christian novelist nowadays is like a man who has found a treasure hidden in the attic of an old house, but he is writing for people who have moved out to the suburbs and who are bloody sick of the old house and everything in it." Somehow, against all odds, Walker Percy got those people to sit up and pay attention. As *Time* put it, "Name another voice in American writing that is as beguiling and civilized as Walker Percy's."

Why read Walker Percy? The answer to that question is the same as the answer to this one: Why understand the twentieth century? Even Percy's harshest critics had to acknowledge his skill as diagnostician, although they deplored his old-fashioned prescription. Percy had a comment on that too. He wondered aloud, "whether, in fact, the preposterousness of Judaeo-Christianity is not in fact an index of the preposterousness of the age."

111

A Whiff of Something Lethal

PART FOUR

Finding GOD Among the Headlines

CHAPTER 23

Russia's Untold Story

All history, once you strip the rind off the kernel, is really spiritual," wrote historian Arnold Toynbee. The recent events in the former Soviet Union demonstrate the truth of his statement. I visited there as part of a delegation of nineteen Christian leaders in the fall of 1991, just after the aborted coup that temporarily deposed Mikhail Gorbachev and just before Boris Yeltsin's ascendance to power. Wherever we went, government officials and private citizens alike affirmed that the true crisis in their nation was moral and spiritual. We heard that opinion expressed so adamantly and so often that I came to see it as the great untold story of Russia.

Almost overnight Russia moved away from an official position of atheism and hostility to religion to become perhaps the most open mission field in the world. Wherever we went, officials invited us to set up exchange programs, relief efforts, study centers, and religious publishing ventures. The Russian leaders voiced a fear of total collapse and anarchy unless their society could find a way to change at the core.

After listening to a parade of politicians and government leaders follow the same script of unvarying politeness and respect for Christianity, it was easy to lose sight of how radically the nation had changed. Russian leaders seemed far more receptive to Christian influence than, say, their counterparts in the United States. Could their predecessors have been so devilish? An unexpected visit from Basil brought a jarring reminder of what life had been like for Christians under the Communist regime.

For years Basil, who lived in Moldavia, had clandestinely tuned in to shortwave programs from the West. Basil first heard a news item about our delegation on Voice of America. Then, incredulous, he listened as the official national radio network gave reports of our meetings with the Parliament and the KGB. The new openness toward religion seemed so inconceivable to Basil that he got on a night train and made the fourteen-hour journey from Moldavia to Moscow in order to see us.

Basil showed up in the lobby early one morning, just as we were gathering to pray and to review the day's schedule. He had broad, hulking shoulders and the rugged, weather-beaten features of a farmer, and he looked ill at ease in a suit and tie. He had a most peculiar smile: two front teeth on the top row were missing, and when he smiled, gold fillings in the back molars gleamed faintly through the gap. He presented us with sacks of gorgeous purple grapes and golden apples, which he had hand-picked and carried on his lap from Moldavia. He asked for five minutes to address us.

When Basil opened his mouth and the first sound came out, I jumped. We were meeting in a small room, and Basil spoke at the decibel level of a freight train. I have never heard a louder voice from any human being. We soon learned why.

In 1962 Basil founded a small publishing company with his own funds. He printed Christian pamphlets, distributing a total of 700,000 before the KGB paid him a visit. They demanded that he stop, and when he refused, they arrested him and sent him to a labor camp. At first Basil was perplexed. Why should he be punished for serving God? Of what use could he be in a labor camp? But then one morning he saw in a flash that God had provided a new opportunity.

Every morning before sunup prisoners from the labor camp had to assemble in an open space for roll call. Camp commanders insisted on strict punctuality from prisoners, but not from guards, and so thousands of prisoners stood outdoors several minutes each morning with nothing to do. Basil, who loved to preach, decided to start a church.

As he was recounting this story in the hotel room, Basil spoke louder and faster, gesturing passionately with his arms like an opera singer. Every few sentences the translator grabbed Basil's flailing arm and asked him to please slow down and lower his voice. Each time Basil apologized, looked down at the floor, and began again in a pianissimo that within three seconds crescendoed to a fortissimo. His voice had no volume control, and the reason traced back to that early morning scene in the labor camp.

> As I look back on my visit, one impression lingers above all others: never in my life have I been among people with a more ravenous appetite for God.

Basil preached daily to a truly captive audience. Typically, he had about two minutes before the guards arrived, rarely as long as five minutes, and as a result it took up to two weeks to deliver a single sermon. He had to shout to be heard by several thousand prisoners, a strain that made him hoarse until his voice adapted. Over the years—ten years in all—of preaching outdoors to thousands, he developed the habit of speaking at top volume and breakneck speed, a habit he could never break.

Basil completed his sentence in 1972 and devoted his energies to building an unregistered church in his village. Sometimes he visited the church among the convicts and, he proudly reported, even today a community of a hundred believers still worships in that labor camp.

Basil's difficulties did not end with his release from prison, though. He told us of harassment by the authorities over his unregistered church, of the threats and public slanders and repeated vandalism of the church building. Finally, after nineteen years, opposition had faded away, and he had just laid the last cement block and covered the church with a roof. He had come to Moscow, he said, to thank us for all we were doing, to bring us fresh fruit from Moldavia, and to ask one of our delegation, Alex Leonovich, to speak at the dedication of his church.

"There were many years when I had no encouragement," Basil said. By now he was weeping openly and his voice cracked but did not drop one decibel. "The words of this man, Brother Leonovich, I carried in my heart. He was the one who encouraged me when my hands were tied behind my back." Basil then reached over, grabbed Alex by the shoulders, and kissed him in the Russian style once, twice, fifteen times—one for each year, he said, that he had waited for Alex to return.

"And now, such changes, I can hardly believe them," Basil said in closing. "We have been through the valley of tears. When Billy Graham came in 1959, they let him appear on a balcony but not speak. To think that you are here in Moscow, the center of unbelief, able to talk and drink tea with the leaders of our country. It is a miracle! Brothers and sisters, be bold! With your wings you are lifting up children of the Lord. Where I come from the believers are praying for you at this minute. We believe your visit will help reach our country for God. God bless you all."

Suddenly, I burned with shame. Here we were: nineteen Christian professionals who made a comfortable living from our faith sitting in one of the most luxurious hotels in Moscow. What did we know about the kind of bedrock faith needed in this nation of people who had endured such suffering? What gave us the right to represent the Basils of Russia before the president and Parliament, let alone the KGB?

We stood and prayed with Basil, and then he left. Later that day Alex Leonovich traded in his airplane ticket, incurring a huge penalty, in order to extend his stay. "How could I possibly turn down Basil's invitation?" he said. Our group went off to be feted in grand style with a banquet at the Ukrainian Embassy, and we did not see Basil again until later in the evening.

I looked forward to the event scheduled for that evening, a visit to the Journalists' Club. The inordinately polite reception we were receiving in Moscow was making me nervous. I knew that an entire atheistic state had not warmed to Christianity overnight, and I longed for a dialogue of true substance. I wanted us to be challenged with hard questions about what difference Christianity could make in a country coming apart at the seams. I could count on cynical, hard-bitten journalists to render such a challenge, I thought.

I thought wrong. This is what happened at the Journalists' Club of Moscow. First, we North American Christians, seated on a spotlighted stage in a small theater, introduced ourselves. Prison ministry executive Ron Nikkel, normally taciturn, was feeling rather expansive. "Winston Churchill said you can judge a society by its prisons," he began. "By that standard, both the USSR and the U.S. are tragedies. Our prisons are awful.

"I have been in prisons all over the world, and have talked to sociologists, behaviorists, and criminal justice experts. None of them know how to get prisoners to change. But we believe—and I have seen abundant proof—that Christ can transform a person from the inside out. Jesus, himself a prisoner, was executed, but he rose again. Now many prisoners are rising again, thanks to him."

The room fell silent, and then these "cynical, hard-bitten journalists" did something I would not have predicted in a thousand years. They broke into loud, prolonged applause. These are the questions they tossed at Ron: "What is this forgiveness? How can we find it? How do you get to know God?" Later, one of the journalists told us that his profession had a special affinity for prisoners, since many had served time themselves. For many decades, prisoners had been the primary carriers of truth in a society based on lies.

Evidently, the journalistic elite of Moscow would not be the ones to challenge our basic Christian beliefs. They seemed far more intent on grasping after them, as if grasping for rare secrets of life that had been concealed for seventy years. After all of us seated onstage had introduced ourselves, the journalists themselves spoke.

Russia's Untold Story

A distinguished-looking silver-haired gentleman stood first, identifying himself as an editor of the *Literary Gazette*, which we knew to be one of the most prestigious journals in Russia. "No doubt you know of the problems in our country," he said. "I tell you, however, that the greatest problem is not that we don't have enough sausages. Far worse, we don't have enough ideas. We don't know what to think. The ground has been pulled out from under us. We thank you deeply for coming to our country and holding before us morality, and hope, and faith. It is beautiful to see you in this place. You represent exactly what we need."

The next speaker was his polar opposite, a dissident who specialized in writing political satire. Slovenly dressed, ungroomed and passionate, with a bald head but spectacular two-inch eyebrows, he looked as if he had stepped straight from a Dostoevsky novel. This character spoke in a voice almost as loud as Basil's. He had a bad stutter—odd to hear in a foreign language—and just as he reached a climactic point he would hang up on a word. "You are our salvation, our only hope!" he shouted. "We had a lawful country, a society with religious beliefs, but that was all destroyed in seventy years. Our souls were su-su-su-sucked out. Truth was de-de-destroyed. In the last stage, which we have just lived through, even the C-C-C-C-C-Communist morale was destroyed."

Next, a beautiful blonde woman wearing a red silk blouse and a leather skirt and matching boots made her way to the aisle. She stood just before the stage, her hands clutching a designer purse. I had not seen such fine clothes in Moscow. My translator whispered to me that she was a popular newscaster—something like the Connie Chung of Russia. "I am so shaken to be here tonight," she said, and then paused a moment to control her voice.

"I am shaking! I feel so blessed to learn that American leaders are concerned with spiritual and moral problems. I am a person educated in religion, and yet I am only on the first step in understanding what is God. So many visitors have come here to make a profit in our country, but I am so thankful that the American intelligentsia care enough to come and meet with people at such important levels over these issues."

She was followed by others who rose to give a similarly embarrassing overassessment of our importance as a delegation. As in previous meetings, we tried to mention flaws in American society and in the American church, but the journalists seemed altogether disinterested in apologies or critiques. They seemed, rather, starved—grievously starved for hope.

I thought of the reception our group might get at the National Press Club in Washington, D.C., the questions we might prompt from the editors of the *New Republic* or *Esquire*. I tried to imagine Connie Chung or Barbara Walters being vulnerable before her peers, as this blonde woman had been. As I was mulling over these thoughts, I noticed in the audience a familiar figure in a funny green suit.

The theater lights had been dimmed for our introductions, but now that the audience was responding other lights were switched on. Sitting in the back row was Basil, he of the foghorn voice and the two-minute church in the Gulag. From then on I kept one eye on Basil, wondering how an ex-convict from Moldavia felt in such an environment, among the celebrities of Moscow.

Whenever someone mentioned the word *God* or *Jesus,* Basil raised both fists over his head, and even from the stage I could almost see the gleam in the gap between his teeth. On the back row, out of view of the audience, Basil was acting as our one-person charismatic cheerleading crew.

For the first time that day I glimpsed our group as Basil saw us: his ambassadors, going where he would not be invited, speaking words he could not always follow, opening doors he had thought were sealed shut forever. We too, those of us who felt so unworthy in his presence that morning, had a role to play. It was to do our part to help guarantee that Basil stay free to worship, inside or outside the camp.

Basil stood for millions of Russian Christians who had lived out their faith in fear and trembling. Incredibly, the tables had turned. Now the journalists of Moscow applauded when they heard stories of converted prisoners, and craved news about God as a dying patient craves a miracle cure. They hung on our words about Christianity as Russian economists hung on words about capitalism, as if we were smuggling in a secret formula from the West that might salvage their land.

We were not bringing imports from the West, however. The God we served had been in Russia all along, worshiped hungrily in the camps and in the unregistered house churches and in the cathedrals the Communists had not razed.

These journalists, all masters of Moscow's cocktail party circuit, had never met a simple saint like Basil. It was our job, quite simply, to introduce them.

The day after our meeting with the journalists, a direct and challenging confrontation with Marxist ideology finally came our way, on a visit to the Academy of Social Sciences. The name is misleading: until the August coup the Academy functioned as the preeminent finishing school for Marxist-Leninist leaders. Raisa Gorbachev once taught there, and many world leaders from the former socialist bloc have studied at this elite school.

Like everything else in Russia, the Academy was undergoing tumultuous change. Until the fall of 1991 it received generous funding from the Communist Party, but shortly before our visit subsidies were abruptly cut off. The Academy's professors, once coddled and privileged, now literally had no idea where their next paychecks would come from. In its scramble to survive, the Academy of Social Sciences was reaching out to Christians, who still had some credibility with a restive populace. The Academy was even negotiating to establish a department for the study of Christianity.

Of all people in Russia, these Academy professors were true believers. Fed Communist theory practically from birth, they had devoted their lives to the propagation of it. One could still see relics of that intense devotion in the quasireligious signs posted around Russia: "Lenin Lived. Lenin Lives. Lenin Will Live." They were not prepared to substitute Jesus for Lenin.

The professors recognized they had lost, perhaps forever, the battle of ideas. The cherished Marxist dream was over. Freedom scared them, and yet they could not deny its benefits. One historian present mentioned the two streams that can issue from a common source of revolution: one leads to free arrangements among citizens, the other leads to absolute power.

"We started with common ideals," he said. "Leaders of both our societies talked about justice and equality and individual rights. Yet somehow you have produced a society that with all its problems still conveys courtesy and civility. Your minorities protest against discrimination—but they do not secede or start civil wars. Somehow, beginning from similar ideals, we here have produced a society of beasts. We have murdered our own citizens in the name of the state. We know that we must move toward liberal democracy, but we don't know how. We no longer know what values to build a society upon."

Most groups we had met with plied us eagerly with questions. The Academy professors seemed more anxious to talk. Listening to them, I felt I was in a political therapy session, nodding my head sympathetically as neurotic clients let long-suppressed anxieties spill out.

In the midst of this genteel discussion, one of the Marxist professors, a specialist in philosophy, rose to his feet and asked for the floor (all other speakers had remained seated). Blotches of red appeared on his face, and as soon as he began speaking, anger gushed forth. Others in the room looked around anxiously, concerned that he was straying from the mannerly dialogue. But there was no stopping this man. He had come to deliver a speech—a diatribe, really—not to fraternize with the enemy.

"We need not have God to have morality!" he said. "Erich Fromm

123

developed a fine morality based on Man with a capital *M*. God is not necessary. Why pretend there is a God?"

The philosopher's volume rose, and his face grew even more flushed. He punctuated the air with his finger as he made each point, and I thought of the paintings of Lenin addressing the workers. I thought, too, of stump preachers in the south where I had grown up. Of course! This man was a fanatic evangelist, the last true-blue, dyed-in-the-wool Marxist in Moscow. He was out to gain converts, and it mattered not at all if he was the last person in the world to believe these things. He was a bitter, wounded atheist, and he seized the chance to strike back.

"Marxism has not failed!" he shouted. "Yes, Stalin made mistakes. Yes, even our beloved Lenin made mistakes. Perhaps even Marx made mistakes. But go back to the young Marx, not the old Marx. There you will find the purity of the socialist vision. There you will find a morality based on Man with the capital *M*. That is what we need. As for Christianity, we already tried that in Russia—for one thousand years we tried it."

The members of our delegation were fidgeting in our seats. Being yelled at by a fanatic is not a pleasant sensation, I realized, and tucked away the thought for further reflection. A few members of our group were whispering to their seatmates, and still others were clearing their throats, ready to jump in with a rebuttal.

The philosopher went on for ten or fifteen minutes until finally the emcee forced him to stop. I sensed in the atmosphere of the room an odd mixture of revenge and embarrassment. The professors waited for our response, and I cringed at the possibilities. Some of us weren't far removed from stump preachers ourselves, I knew, and the last thing the Academy needed was a wounded evangelical doing battle with a wounded atheist. By the providence of God, it was Kent Hill who got the floor.

Kent Hill looks more professorial than the professors. He wears glasses, has a scholarly demeanor, and speaks in soft, measured tones, the epitome of rational discourse. He also has a Ph.D. in Russian studies, and had taught at Seattle Pacific University before taking the position of president of the Institute on Religion and Democracy in Washington, D.C. I did not envy him the spotlight he had just stepped into, but I could not imagine a finer representative to respond on our behalf.

"First, I want to affirm your right to your beliefs," Kent began, and waited respectfully for his Russian translator. "I am concerned about intolerance in Russia today—intolerance of atheists. I recently learned of an incident where a group allowed a Christian believer to speak, but shouted down an atheist. We have not come in that spirit. We support freedom of religion, and that includes freedom for those who do not believe in God."

Tension rushed from the room as if someone had opened an air lock. The professors nodded approval, and even the philosopher gave a curt nod. Kent continued.

"The issues you have raised tonight, sir, are important issues. In fact, I cannot think of more important issues to discuss. You have touched on questions of ultimate meaning for humanity and for the universe. Our group has thought long and hard about these questions. We have reached some conclusions, and we would love to discuss those with you.

"But one night's discussion would hardly do justice to these issues. I do not feel comfortable presenting a brief response. Could I make a suggestion? My family and I are moving to Moscow in December, and I will be teaching a course in Christian apologetics at Moscow State University. I will gladly return to your Academy with Christian friends and set up a forum in which we can consider these important matters."

Again, nods of approval all around. Kent resumed, "But since I have the floor, I would like to mention why I believe the way I do." At this point, Kent shocked everyone by lapsing into fluent Russian. The professors removed their headphones, and now we Americans were the ones listening to the simultaneous translation.

Kent told of a time of doubt in his life when he was tempted to abandon his Christian beliefs. He began reading Dostoevsky's great novel

The Brothers Karamazov—at this mention, more nods—which deals with many of the issues raised by the Academy philosopher.

"At first I found myself attracted to Ivan, the agnostic. His arguments against God were powerful, especially those concerning the problem of evil. I sensed in him a sincerity and a brilliant mind. As I read Dostoevsky's book, I found myself gradually losing faith. But to my surprise, I was eventually won over by the love shown by Ivan's brother Alyosha. Ivan had fine arguments, but he had no love. He could reason his way to a morality, but he could not create the love necessary to fulfill it. Eventually, I came to believe in Christ because I found in him a source for that love."

With that, Kent Hill sat down, and our meeting with the Academy of Social Sciences was transformed.

It occurred to me as we drove away from the ghostly marble buildings that Kent Hill had done far more than defuse one awkward confrontation. He had given us a model of evangelism for Russia, perhaps the only model that will authentically work. First, he had begun with a genuine respect for the Russian's own beliefs, even those diametrically opposed to his own. Unlike the philosophy professor, he had listened with courtesy and compassion before speaking.

Next, by moving to Moscow, Kent had committed himself to incarnational ministry. By themselves, no delegations of foreigners visiting for a week or a month will bring long-term change to the country. But a sprinkling of dedicated people who share the hardships and the turmoil, people willing to stand in the Moscow bread lines, could perhaps become the salt that savors the whole society.

Finally, Kent pointed to the source of truth latent in the Russian culture itself. His lapse into the Russian language, almost instinctive as his response turned personal, and his reference to Dostoevsky communicated far more to that audience than if he had quoted an entire epistle from the New Testament.

It was also through reading Dostoevsky, Aleksandr Solzhenitsyn reports, that he first began to understand the primacy of the spiritual over the material. That led the way to a conversion experience in a labor camp that changed the course of his life and ultimately affected the course of his nation. Solzhenitsyn, too, became a directional signal pointing the way back toward God. As Kent Hill had so gently revealed, the seeds of renewal already lay in Russian soil.

In *Crime and Punishment* Dostoevsky writes of the perilous sensation of living on one square yard of a cliff, on a narrow ledge where two feet can hardly stand, surrounded on all sides by an abyss, the ocean, everlasting darkness, everlasting solitude, and an everlasting storm. A good image for modern Russia, I decided. Everyone knows the danger on all sides; no one knows how to get off the cliff.

What went wrong in the former Soviet Union? The news media focus on a fatally flawed economic system. Curiously, I have not seen one mention in the media of what every Russian leader insisted to us: the grave crisis is not economic or political, but rather moral and spiritual. The failure of Marxism, we were told again and again, is above all a theological failure.

In his Templeton Address in 1983, Solzhenitsyn said:

> Over half a century ago, while I was still a child, I recall hearing a number of older people offer the following explanation for the great disasters that had befallen Russia: "Men have forgotten God; that's why all this has happened." Since then I have spent well-nigh fifty years working on the history of our revolution; in the process I have read hundreds of books, collected hundreds of personal testimonies, and have already contributed eight volumes of my own toward the effort of clearing away the rubble left by that upheaval. But if I were asked today to formulate as concisely as possible the main cause of the ruinous revolution that swallowed up some sixty million

of our people, I could not put it more accurately than to repeat: "Men have forgotten God; that's why all this has happened."

Solzhenitsyn went on to say, "I myself see Christianity today as the only living spiritual force capable of undertaking the spiritual healing of Russia." When he made those remarks, the USSR was still a superpower, and Solzhenitsyn was widely assailed for his old-fashioned views. Now, less than a decade later our delegation heard almost the identical assessment from top leaders of the nation. Above any other nation, the Soviet Union endeavored to get along without God. "Religion will disappear," Marx flatly predicted, its quaint beliefs made obsolete by the New Socialist Man. But religion did not disappear, and no New Socialist Man emerged.

In this century a morality play has been conducted on a grand scale, with catastrophic consequences. What lies ahead? On the airplane on the way home, various members of our delegation tried to speculate. We all sensed the enormity of change that has already come. The new openness toward religion exceeded what any of us might have hoped for. In that regard, the prayers of millions of Christians both inside and outside Russia have been answered.

I, too, sensed the epic, and yet I confess that I tend toward realism, and hope does not come easily for me. I can hardly envision what a restored, much less redeemed, Russia would look like.

One thing only gives me hope. I will never forget the expressions on the faces of Basil, and the blonde television newscaster, and even the vice-chairman of the KGB. Jesus' parables about the kingdom and the fig tree and the great banquet make one truth explicit: God goes where he is wanted. He does not force himself on an individual or on a nation, whether it be first-century Jews or twentieth-century Americans. And as I look back on my visit to Russia, one impression lingers above all others: never in my life have I been among people with a more ravenous appetite for God.

CHAPTER 24

The God That Failed

Since my trip to Russia, I have thought much about the Marxist experiment that Russians now call "seventy-four years on the road to nowhere." Why did it fail so badly? Perhaps the best answer to that question came during a meeting between our group of Christians and the editors of *Pravda*, formerly the official mouthpiece of the Communist Party.

One sample quotation from *Pravda* in 1950 shows how the newspaper got its reputation as a propaganda organ: "If you meet with difficulties in your work, or suddenly doubt your abilities, think of him—of Stalin—and you will find the confidence you need. If you feel tired in an hour when you should not, think of him—of Stalin—and your work will go well. If you are seeking a correct decision, think of him—of Stalin—and you will find that decision."

The Russians used to have a cynical saying about their two largest newspapers: "There is no *pravda* [truth] in *Izvestia* [news] and no *izvestia* in *Pravda*." Ever since 1989, like everything else in Russia, *Pravda* has undergone tumultuous change. For a time Boris Yeltsin shut it down. When we visited, in the fall of 1991, circulation figures were in a tailspin that signified Communism's fall from grace: daily circulation had declined from 11 million to 700,000.

The editors of *Pravda* seemed earnest, sincere, searching—and shaken to the core. So shaken that they were now asking for help from emissaries of a religion their founder had scorned as "the opiate of the people." The editors remarked wistfully that Christianity and Communism have many of the same ideals: equality, sharing, justice, and racial

129

harmony. Yet they had to admit the Marxist pursuit of that vision had produced the worst nightmares the world has ever seen. Why?

Sociologists, philosophers, and economists will no doubt pronounce their own postmortems over Marxism, but what struck me during the ensuing discussion is that Communism failed because of two basic errors in what theologians call *anthropology,* or "the doctrine of humanity."

First, Communists ignored our fallen nature. Early Communists had promised the emergence of a new breed of human being. Leon Trotsky wrote in 1924, "Man will become immeasurably stronger, wiser and subtler; his body will become more harmonized, his movements more rhythmic, his voice more musical. The forms of life will become dynamically dramatic. The average human type will rise to the heights of an Aristotle, a Goethe or a Marx. And above this ridge new peaks will rise." Today, any Russian would laugh out loud at Trotsky's prediction.

Classical Marxists fought fiercely against religion for a shrewd reason: In order to motivate workers to rise up violently against their oppressors, Marxists had to kill off any hope in a heavenly life beyond this one, and any fear of divine punishment. They had to replace a God-man with a man-God. But human beings are fallen creatures, not man-Gods. It was for this reason that no New Socialist Man ever emerged.

Two decades ago, when Communism still posed a worldwide threat, a Romanian pastor named Josif Tson wrote of the contradiction that lies at the heart of a Marxist view of humanity:

> [They teach] their pupils that life is the product of chance combinations of matter, that it is governed by Darwinian laws of adaptation and survival, and that it is man's only chance. There is no after-life, no "savior" to reward self-sacrifice or to punish egoism or rapacity. After the pupils have been thus

taught, I am sent in to teach them to be noble and honorable men and women, expending all their energies on doing good for the benefit of society, even to the point of self-sacrifice. They must be courteous, tell only the truth, and live a morally pure life. But they lack motivation for goodness. They see that in a purely material world only he who hurries and grabs for himself possesses anything. Why should they be self-denying and honest? What motive can be offered them to live lives of usefulness to others?

> The editors of *Pravda* seemed earnest, sincere, searching—and shaken to the core.

The *Pravda* editors conceded to us that they did not know how to motivate people to show compassion. A recent campaign to raise funds for the children of Chernobyl had foundered. The average Soviet citizen would rather spend his money on drink than support needy children. Their own polls had revealed that 70 percent of Soviet parents would not allow their children to have contact with a disabled child; 80 percent would not give money to help; some advocated infanticide. "How do you reform, change, motivate people?" the editors asked us.

The editors' question points to the second major flaw in Marxist anthropology. Early Communists believed that they—not God—were the ones to determine morality, which could then be enforced from the top down. Seventy-four years of Communism proved beyond all doubt that goodness cannot be legislated from the Kremlin and enforced at the point of a gun. In a great irony, attempts to compel morality tend to produce rebellious subjects and tyrannical rulers.

Worse, the Communist rulers who made decisions about morality tragically recapitulated the first flaw: they, too, were fallen creatures. Moral principles shifted depending on who was in power. *Pravda* was now showing admirable compassion by raising funds for the victims of the Chernobyl disaster. But the same newspaper had, for example, shown no compassion whatever for the children victims of Stalin's enforced starvation of the Ukraine. What "higher law" determined when compassion applied and when it did not? *Pravda* had no answer.

I came away from Russia with the strong sense that we Christians would do well to relearn basic lessons of theology. Some of my friends seem almost embarrassed by doctrines like the Fall and original sin. "Christianity has such a pessimistic view of human nature," they say.

Others wish that God would play a more heavy-handed role in human affairs. "He allows too much freedom," they say. "Why doesn't God interfere more? Why does he let so much evil go unpunished in this life?"

In Russia I saw the tragic results of the alternatives—an optimistic view of human nature and a morality based on compulsion, not inner transformation. It was a darkly sobering reminder of what happens when human beings ignore God's revelation and come up with their own.

CHAPTER 25

The Wall Comes Tumbling Down

T
he reason formerly Communist countries so quickly opened their doors to Christians after the collapse of Marxism traces back to the testimony of Christians who stayed faithful to their calling. They, too, are part of the untold story.

In East Germany, one of the few Eastern European countries with a Protestant majority, for forty years the church sought ways to serve the "city of God" while living in an officially atheistic "city of the world." Since many avenues (such as television and radio) were closed, early on the church adopted a commitment to care for the neediest members of society, especially the profoundly disabled. And they met together regularly for worship and prayer.

Although Jesus spoke of a "kingdom that is within you," throughout history the church has faced a constant temptation to form alliances with external centers of power. The U.S. church faces just that temptation today, with its emphasis on politics rather than spirituality. Yet, in a nation like East Germany under Communism, that possibility did not exist. Christians there had no "power base" as such, none but the power of love and prayer.

Yet, against all odds, when the decisive moment for change finally arrived in the Eastern Bloc, the church led the way in a peaceful revolution. East Germans look back on October 9, 1989, as *die Wende*, the "turning point." The crucial event took place, appropriately enough, in Leipzig, a bastion of the Reformation where Luther preached in the sixteenth century and Bach played the organ in the eighteenth.

During 1989 four churches in Leipzig (including Bach's *Thomaskirche*) were holding weekly prayer meetings every Monday evening at 5:00. The prayer meetings had begun seven years before, in 1982, when Pastor Christian Fuehrer invited his parishioners to gather to pray for peace. The pastors conducted the old Lutheran hymns, addressed their congregations with the Bible in one hand and the daily newspaper in the other, and led rounds of prayer. In this way, they tried to give meaning and hope to the beleaguered East Germans. At first, a handful of Christians, a few dozen at most, assembled.

Gradually, though, the congregations for these prayer meetings began to swell, attracting not just faithful Christians but also political dissidents and ordinary citizens. The church was the one place where the Communist state allowed freedom of assembly. After each meeting the groups would join together and walk through the dark streets of the old city, holding candles and banners—a most benign form of political protest. Virtually every protest demonstration in the entire country began in this way, with worship.

Eventually, news media from the West picked up the story. Alarmed, the Communist hierarchy debated how to stamp out the peaceful marches. Secret police surrounded the churches, sometimes roughing up the marchers. But the crowds in Leipzig kept growing: hundreds, thousands, then 50,000.

Pastor Wonneberger of the Saint Nikolai Church found himself in an unexpected role as de facto leader of the movement. He preached peace and gave practical advice on techniques of nonviolence even as the secret police phoned in death threats and posted lookouts around his church.

On October 9, nearly everyone expected the political pressure to reach a critical mass. East Berlin was celebrating the forty-year anniversary of the Communist state, and viewed the marches in Leipzig as a provocation. Police and army units moved into Leipzig in force, and East German leader Erich Honecker gave them instructions to shoot the demonstrators. The country braced for a replay of Tiananmen Square. Leipzig's Lutheran bishop warned of a massacre, hospitals cleared emergency rooms, and churches and concert halls agreed to open their doors in case demonstrators needed quick refuge.

When time came for prayer meeting at Nikolai Church, two thousand Communist Party members rushed inside to occupy all the seats. The church simply opened its seldom-used balconies, and a thousand protestors also crowded inside. The *Christian Century* reports that the service itself was a turning point: Party members who attended with the intention of disrupting things realized for the first time that the church was indeed working for peaceful change.

No one knows for sure why the military held their fire that night. Egon Krenz, the short-lived successor to Honecker, took personal credit for rescinding the order. Some theorize that Mikhail Gorbachev himself telephoned a warning to Honecker. Others believe the army was simply cowed by the huge crowds. But everyone credits the prayer vigils in Leipzig for kindling the process of momentous change. In the end, 70,000 people marched peacefully through downtown Leipzig. The following Monday, 120,000 marched. A week later, 500,000 turned out—nearly the entire population of Leipzig.

In early November the largest march of all took place, almost one million people marching peacefully through East Berlin. Erich Honecker resigned, humiliated. Police refused to fire on the demonstrators. At midnight on November 9, something no one had even dared pray for happened: a gap opened up in the hated Berlin Wall. East Germans streamed through the checkpoints, past guards who had always obeyed orders to "shoot to kill." Not a single life was lost as throngs of people marching with candles brought down a government.

Like a windstorm of pure air driving out pollution, the peaceful revolution spread across the globe. In 1989 alone ten nations comprising more than half a billion people—Poland, East Germany, Hungary, Czechoslovakia, Bulgaria, Romania, Albania, Yugoslavia, Mongolia, the Soviet Union—experienced nonviolent revolutions.

As Bud Bultman, a producer and writer for CNN, wrote: "We in the media watched in astonishment as the walls of totalitarianism came crashing down. But in the rush to cover the cataclysmic events, the story behind the story was overlooked. We trained our cameras on hundreds of thousands of people praying for freedom, votive candles in hand, and yet we missed the transcendent dimension, the explicitly spiritual and religious character of the story. We looked right at it and could not see it."

Some did see it. East Germans still speak of those days as a miracle. "Whether or not prayers really move mountains, they certainly mobilized the population of Leipzig," reported the *New Republic.* "To hear them sing 'A Mighty Fortress Is Our God' is enough to make you believe it." Several weeks after the October 9 turning point, a huge banner appeared across a Leipzig street: *Wir danken Dir, Kirche* (We thank you, church).

CHAPTER 26

The Unlikely Prophet of Prague

Without doubt, the one great star who has arisen from Eastern Europe is Václav Havel, president of the Czech Republic. Several decades ago, he gained a reputation as an absurdist writer of plays, in the tradition of Franz Kafka. Then, when his plays began attacking the Communist government directly, he assumed the mantle of a dissident intellectual. For more than two decades, Havel's plays, essays, and books were banned in Czechoslovakia. Indicted for crimes of subversion and "hooliganism," he was sentenced to prison, and it was there that he developed a profoundly moral—even spiritual—vision for his country.

Havel's vision seemed hopelessly fantastical during the long, oppressive years of Soviet occupation. But in 1989 Czechoslovakia, too, shed the yoke of Communism, and the newly free country turned to Václav Havel for leadership. Why would an artist and intellectual, a hero of dissidents, choose to dirty his hands in politics? Havel himself answers that question: "I once asked a friend of mine, a wonderful man and a wonderful writer, to fill a certain political post. He refused, arguing that someone had to remain independent. I replied that if you all said that, it could happen in the end, no one will be independent, because there won't be anyone around to make that independence possible and stand behind it."

More successfully than any leader of a former Communist country, Havel has led his country down the road of independence. The process has not been without pain. To his deep disappointment, Havel had to grant the Slovaks' request to secede, effectively dismembering his nation. He resigned his post, and was promptly reelected president of the newly formed Czech Republic.

Contrary to most politicians, Havel has always insisted on absolute honesty. For a time, he appeared on a weekly television program in which he answered whatever questions callers would ask. Many nights he can be found in local restaurants and pubs, clad in blue jeans, ready to engage his citizens in dialogue. And Havel has argued persuasively for a deeper dimension to politics.

No speech better summarizes Havel's commitment to truth and transcendent values than the inaugural address he gave on New Year's Day 1990, his first public address to Czechoslovakia. Selected portions of that speech follow.

"For the past forty years on this day you have heard the same thing, with variations, from the mouths of my predecessors: that our country is flourishing; that so many million tons of steel have been produced; that all of us are happy; that we trusted our Government; and that beautiful prospects were opening up before us.

"I imagine that you did not propose that I should take this office to hear similar lies from me.

"Our country is not flourishing. The great creative and spiritual potential of our two nations is not being meaningfully exploited. Whole branches of industry are producing products in which nobody is interested while we have shortages of products we need. The state, which is called the workers' state, has been humiliating and exploiting the workers.

"We have spoiled the soil, the rivers, and the forests inherited from our ancestors, and today we have got the worst environment in the whole of Europe. In our country life expectancy is lower than in most European countries. . . . The existing regime, armed by its haughty and intolerant ideology, degraded man into a unit of production and nature into a production tool. Thus it attacked their very nature and the mutual relationship between them.

"... None of this is the main thing. The worst is that we are living in a ruined moral climate. We have been taken ill morally because we have grown accustomed to say one thing and think another. We have learned to believe nothing, to pay no attention to each other, to care only for ourselves. Concepts like love, friendship, compassion, humility, or forgiveness have lost their range and content. For many of us, these signify only a kind of psychological eccentricity or appear as greetings which have strayed in from the past, now somewhat ridiculous in the era of computers and space rockets.

> Somehow Václav Havel has gotten reelected by telling the truth.

"... The most recent past—and especially the last six weeks of our peaceful revolution—have proved how great has been our human, moral, and spiritual change and how great a civic culture slumbered in our society under the imposed veil of apathy.... Everywhere in the world people are surprised at our marvelous strength to shrug the totalitarian system off our shoulders within a few weeks in a decent and peaceful way. ... We ourselves are surprised. And we ask from where our young people, who have never known any other system, drew their longing for truth, their free thought, their political information. ...

"I think that this hopeful aspect of our situation today has two main sources. A man is never a product of the external world only but is always capable of relating himself to something beyond, despite a systematic attempt to eradicate this capacity by the external world.

"Secondly, those humanistic and democratic traditions, which were so often idly spoken about, were sleeping somewhere in the subconscious and were transferred from one generation to another to be recovered by each of us at a correct moment and transferred into action. . . .

"Our first President has written: 'Jesus not Caesar.' . . . Today this idea has again been revived in ourselves. I dare say that perhaps we even have the possibility of spreading it further and thus to bring it as a new element into European and world politics. If we want it, the love, the longing for understanding, spiritual and intellectual strength can permanently radiate outwards from our country. This is what we can offer as our individual contribution to world politics. . . .

"We are a small country but despite that we used to be the spiritual crossroads of Europe. Why should we not become this crossroads again? Would this not be another contribution to repay others for the assistance we shall need from them?"

Havel went on to mention a specific political platform: to bring about fair and peaceful elections; to support better conditions for children, old people, women, the sick, and weakened members of society; and to announce a broad amnesty for prisoners. "I ask the public not to be afraid of the discharged prisoners, not to embitter their lives, but to help them in the Christian spirit, after their return among us, to find in themselves what prisons failed to produce: repentance and the longing to live properly."

The rich ironies of Havel's speech have stayed with me ever since I read it. First, I was struck by the startling honesty of the speech itself. I could not imagine an American politician delivering anything comparable. Cynically, I wondered how long it will take these fledgling politicians in Eastern Europe to learn that the usual goal of democracy is not truth but rather reelection. Yet somehow Václav Havel gets reelected by telling the truth.

The spiritual ironies are even greater than the political. A man who got his reputation as a playwright in the theater of the absurd was in effect pledging to lead his nation in a spiritual renewal based on Christian values. Czech citizens were celebrating in the streets because for the first time in four decades Christian services were being broadcast on state television and Christmas carols played on radio (this while American courts were solemnly considering the legality of Christmas crèches in town squares).

Havel's search for high moral ground did not end with his inaugural address. He constantly reminds fellow Czechs of their opportunity to serve as the spiritual crossroads of Europe. He is one of the few European leaders who have consistently called for intervention to stop the slaughter in the former Yugoslavia. When he visited the United States and addressed a rare joint session of Congress, his speech sounded more like a sermon than a political speech.

Havel admits that he has not yet worked out his religious faith. He believes that "all of this—life and the universe—is not just 'in and of itself.' I believe that nothing disappears forever, and less so our deeds. . . . I try to live in the spirit of Christian morality, but that doesn't mean that I'm a genuinely believing Christian."

141

Havel is still groping toward God. He does not pray or worship regularly, and yet he poignantly recalls taking part in secret masses in prison. He cannot envision a personal God, and cannot "fully, inwardly" accept Christ as the Son of God. Yet he believes in transcendence, as he defines it in this way: "That there is a great mystery above me which is the focus of all meaning and the highest moral authority; that the event called the 'world' has a deeper order and meaning, and therefore is more than just a cluster of improbable accidents; that in my own life I am reaching for something that goes far beyond me and the horizon of the world that I know; that in everything I do I touch eternity in a strange way."

So far, Havel has proven better at diagnosis than at cure. His plays, his essays, and his speeches all point to the spiritual sickness of modern civilization. More forcefully than any other world leader, he can articulate the poverty of life without transcendence, the loss of metaphysical uncertainty, the chaos of morality without a moral authority. "We are going through a great departure from God which has no parallel in history," he says, sounding like Solzhenitsyn as he identifies atheism as the root of modern crisis.

Spiritual renewal, Havel admits, is not something that will drop out of heaven into our laps; "it is a task that confronts us all, every moment of our existence." Publicly, courageously, at times profoundly, Václav Havel is confronting that task on the world stage.

CHAPTER 27

Hearing Screams

Shortly after the Iron Curtain fell, Oleg Gordievsky, the most senior Soviet agent ever to work for the West, published his memoirs, *KGB: The Inside Story*. They included Gordievsky's recollections of Whittaker Chambers and Alger Hiss, the two principal witnesses in a series of congressional hearings and court trials as famous in their day (1948–50) as Watergate was in more recent times.

After thirteen years as a loyal Communist, Whittaker Chambers abruptly left the party in 1938, naming Alger Hiss as one of his accomplices in espionage. It was a serious charge: Hiss, a high official in the State Department, went on to counsel President Roosevelt at Yalta and was instrumental in the founding of the United Nations. Some ten years later, Chambers's allegations surfaced sensationally in congressional hearings, giving a huge boost to the careers of Richard Nixon, J. Edgar Hoover, and Joseph McCarthy.

In court, Chambers produced microfilm evidence to back up his charge, and a jury convicted Alger Hiss. Yet Hiss adamantly insisted on his innocence, and eventually attracted much sympathy from those who saw him as a victim of a McCarthy-era witch-hunt. After spending time in jail, he became the first lawyer ever readmitted to the Massachusetts bar following a major criminal conviction. Meanwhile, Hiss sympathizers painted Chambers as a vengeful scaremonger who had ruined a fine man's career. Chambers wrote articles for *National Review* for a while, worked as an editor for *Time*, then retired to a farm in Maryland, and finally died with few friends and a soiled reputation.

But now Gordievsky, a KGB mole writing forty years after the events, has endorsed Chambers's version. On a whim, I decided to look up the eight-hundred-page autobiography, *Witness*, that Chambers claimed to have written for his children in order to explain his actions which so many had misconstrued. I was interested less in his rationale for informing on Hiss than in his motives for defecting from Communism. Was his early disillusion an advance echo of what would reverberate throughout the Communist world in the early 1990s?

Witness records step by step Chambers's pilgrimage first toward and then away from Communism. Originally, he had found in the party the two certainties "for which the mind of man tirelessly seeks: a reason to live and a reason to die." At considerable personal risk, he had gone underground to head a Washington spy ring because he truly believed Marxism represented the last great hope on earth.

Why did that hope crumble? Chambers quotes the daughter of a German diplomat who had lived in Moscow, trying to explain why her father had suddenly turned against Communism: "He was immensely pro-Soviet, and then one night in Moscow he heard screams. That's all. Simply one night he heard screams."

For Chambers, the first scream came in the form of a ten-line newspaper report about the death of Dmitri Schmidt, a Red Army general shot for treason. Chambers had ignored all rumors about the purges taking place in Moscow, but for some reason the report of this one man's death got through to him. He saw that the killing would go on and on. "How long are you going to keep on killing people?" Lady Astor once asked Stalin. "As long as it is necessary," he replied.

At about this time Chambers was sitting in his apartment in Baltimore watching his daughter in her high chair.

> She was the most miraculous thing that had ever happened in my life. I liked to watch her even when she smeared porridge on her face or dropped it meditatively on the floor. My eye

came to rest on the delicate convolutions of her ear—those intricate, perfect ears. The thought passed through my mind: "No, those ears were not created by any chance coming together of atoms in nature (the Communist view). They could have been created only by immense design." The thought was involuntary and unwanted. I crowded it out of my mind. But I never wholly forgot it or the occasion. . . . I did not then know that, at that moment, the finger of God was first laid upon my forehead.

> The turning point came when Chambers at last acknowledged that every human being— his daughter, the Red Army general— must have a soul.

The turning point came when Chambers at last acknowledged that every human being—his daughter, the Red Army general—must have a soul. Either individual human beings have inherent worth, bestowed by a Creator, or we are mere animals, subject only to the laws we forcibly impose on one another. Materialists denied the soul and exalted the mind of man, but Chambers had seen from the inside the end product of their vision of a world "liberated" from God: "Man cannot organize the world for himself without God; without God man can only organize the world *against man*. The gas ovens of Buchenwald and the Communist execution cellars exist first within our minds."

At last, the thought struck him, "This is evil, absolute evil. Of this evil I am a part."

Later, reading Victor Hugo's *Les Miserables*, Chambers encountered a faith that combined two seeming irreconcilables: Christianity and revolution. The novel showed him the possibility of a revolution imposed not from above, at the point of a gun barrel, but rather from below: a revolution of Christians offering service to the poor, the sick, the dying, the lonely children, in the slums and prisons and sewers of Paris. Hugo's vision, Chambers confessed, "did not correspond to anything I knew as Christian in the world about me. But it corresponded exactly to a need I felt within myself."

Next came the journal of George Fox and the quiet presence of a group of Quakers who taught Chambers to pray and taught him also the (to him) alien virtue of humility. Chambers often reflected on a line of Charles Péguy, "No one is so competent a witness to the substance of Christianity as the sinner; no one, except, perhaps, the saint." Whittaker Chambers, who had seen both, came away convinced of Christianity's truth.

Chambers died in 1961, a sad and mistrusted man. His book, its title ironically echoing Péguy, mostly gathers dust on library shelves. Until the publication of Gordievsky's book last year, the media rarely mentioned the name of this man who had dominated headlines four decades before.

I could not help thinking, though, as I read Chambers's book, that he served as a kind of forerunner of what has transpired on a global scale. Economics alone cannot account for the sea change that has taken place before our eyes. Communists in places like East Germany, Latvia, Russia, and even Albania and Bulgaria have abandoned a vision of the world that once they would have died for.

Why? First, they heard screams. The wilderness prophets who cried out, like Solzhenitsyn, could not be silenced. Finally, the authorities themselves had to recognize the bankruptcy of a system based on humanity alone.

Almost forty years ago Chambers wrote,

> Political freedom, as the Western world has known it, is only a
> political reading of the Bible. The crisis of Communism exists
> to the degree in which it has failed to free the peoples it rules

from God. . . . Economics is not the central problem of this century. It is a relative problem which can be solved in relative ways. Faith is the central problem of this age. The Western world does not know it, but it already possesses the answer to this problem—but only provided that its faith in God and the freedom He enjoins is as great as Communism's faith in Man.

All over this planet, dedicated Communists have lost faith in humanity. Will they, like Chambers, take the further step of discovering faith in God? If so—irony of ironies—can they reteach it to the West?

147

CHAPTER 28

Big Nanny Is Watching

Polish playwright Janusz Glowacki recalls visiting a "This Is America" exhibit in Warsaw during the darkest days of Stalinism. While listening to a decadent boogie-woogie soundtrack, he gravely filed past displays of loud ties, gaudy billboards, KKK crosses, and even insects from Colorado that were supposedly dropped from planes at night to devour socialists' potatoes.

"The exhibition was meant to evoke horror, disgust, and hatred," Glowacki writes. "It had, however, the opposite effect. Thousands of Varsovians, dressed in their holiday best, waited every day in lines as long as those to see Lenin's Tomb and in solemn silence looked at the display, listened respectfully to the boogie-woogie, wanting in this way, at least, to manifest their blind and hopeless love for the United States."

Now, several years after the astonishing changes in Europe, Poles and even Russians can freely design their own loud ties and gaudy billboards and compose their own boogie-woogie. Against all odds, Western culture has triumphed, with very few shots being fired. The Cold War is over; the Red Threat has vanished. Now what? With the U.S. no longer defining its identity in opposition to Communism, what lies ahead?

Author Neil Postman *(Amusing Ourselves to Death)* suggests that though we seem to have escaped George Orwell's *1984*, we are still in dire peril from Aldous Huxley's *Brave New World*. People often confuse those two books, but they present quite different visions of the future. Maybe it's not Big Brother we should fear, but Big Nanny.

Orwell warned against an external enemy that relies on violence and propaganda to impose its will—something like Communism or Nazism, both of which Orwell knew well. In contrast, Huxley warned against a more subtle enemy from within. People will gladly trade away their freedom and autonomy for a technology that promises comfort, safety, and amusement, he predicted. Orwell's villains used a pain machine to enforce their decrees; Huxley's villains relied on pleasure. Orwell's regime banned books; in Huxley's fantasy, books are plentiful, but no one wants to read them.

Since 1984 has come and gone, with its threat fast receding, perhaps it is time to update Huxley's gentle nightmare. What would a "Brave New Society" look like?

1. *A Brave New Society repairs the defects in human personality.* Neurophysiologist José M. R. Delgado made a splash a few years back when he brought a charging bull to a dead stop by pressing the small button of a radio transmitter. (He had implanted an electrode in the bull's brain.) The title of his book describing this and other experiments says it well: *Physical Control of the Mind: Toward a Psychocivilized Society.*

Open the spigot of government funds, say the behavioral scientists, and we will identify the physiological bases of violence, addictions, and sexual and personality disorders. Then we can repair them through drugs or surgery.

Admittedly, a defect-free society may forfeit some valuable contributions from deviants. Would Beethoven, Schubert, and Brahms have created such music if their personality disorders had been repaired? We may have lost Jerome's Vulgate translation of the Bible, which served the church for one thousand years (he worked on it as a means of sublimating sexual desire), and Augustine may have watered down his *Confessions*. But just think how Abraham Lincoln—who rarely smiled, struggled with depression, and was married to a probable psychopath—might have been "improved."

2. *A Brave New Society simplifies morality.* For centuries, church and state have hacked their way through a thicket of issues relating to sexuality and social justice. The New Society dispenses with such notions as absolute truth and "inalienable rights." Only two principles matter: kindness and tolerance.

Politically correct thinking, based on kindness and tolerance, will insist on certain cultural adjustments. *Huckleberry Finn* and the Brothers Grimm will need a complete reworking. Anti-Semitic passages in Shakespeare must be excised. Can a Politically Correct Bible be far behind? (Zacchaeus was, after all, not "short," but "vertically challenged.")

> Since 1984 has come and gone, perhaps it is time to update Aldous Huxley's gentle nightmare.

151

3. *A Brave New Society solves problems through technology.* C. S. Lewis wrote, "For the wise men of old, the cardinal problem of human life was how to conform the soul to objective reality, and the solution was wisdom, self-discipline, and virtue. For the modern mind, the cardinal problem is how to subdue reality to the wishes of man, and the solution is a technique."

We apply the criteria "developed, less-developed, underdeveloped," to Brave New Societies, avoiding such value-laden words as *just, moral, good.* Sad-eyed prophets like Solzhenitsyn used to argue that the suffering East could teach spiritual values to the materialistic West. I haven't heard that argument lately; the East is too busy trying to catch up to the economic standards of the West.

Africa and parts of Asia seem beyond our technological capacity to fix. They'll have their place in the Brave New Society, too: we'll watch two-minute reports on the devastation, sandwiched in between the sports and weather. Such an attitude has good precedent, dating back at least to Boccaccio's *Decameron*. During the Black Death, some young men and women took refuge in a well-protected castle. While carts gathered up the dead outside, these fortunate few devoted themselves to pleasure and games, telling the famous stories imagined by Boccaccio.

4. A Brave New Society elevates entertainment above all other values. To get a measure of how much we value entertainment, consider that a good baseball pitcher earns twice as much for nine innings' work as a high school physics teacher earns in a year.

George Orwell feared a Big Brother whose projected image would intrude in every home. The screens are in place now, but we choose the images we want, and the bottom line is entertainment. As media scholar David Thorburn puts it, we can only stand in awe of "television's genius for marketing banality."

American families watch television five to seven hours a day, demonstrating an obsession with entertainment unmatched in history. Naturally, the medium affects the message. Watch *Sesame Street* for three minutes and you'll see what education looks like when forced through an entertainment grid. Or compare the successful televangelist programs with the average local church service.

I am reminded of a quote from Henry David Thoreau, who had a disturbingly stunted view: "Our inventions are wont to be pretty toys, which distract our attention from serious things. They are but improved means to an unimproved end, an end which it was already but too easy to arrive at. . . . We are in great haste to construct a magnetic telegraph from Maine to Texas; but Maine and Texas, it may be, have nothing important to communicate."

How close are we to achieving the Brave New Society? A recent visit to the British Museum Library gave me pause. One room displays original letters and manuscript pages from great authors, arranged chronologically. I spent several hours there, proceeding from Shakespeare and Donne to Elizabeth Barrett Browning and Jane Austen and Virginia Woolf. Finally, I reached the most recent manuscript collection. There, displayed in a formal wooden case with gold leaf lettering, was the scrawled original of one of the most famous songs of this half-century: "Oh yeah, oh yeah, I wanna hold your hand." The poet had captured the spirit of the age precisely.

Daniel Boorstin, former Librarian of Congress and director of the Smithsonian National Museum of American History, offers this assessment of contemporary culture:

> When we pick up our newspaper at breakfast, we expect—we even demand—that it bring us momentous events since the night before. We turn on the car radio as we drive to work and expect "news" to have occurred since the morning newspaper went to press. Returning in the evening, we expect our house not only to shelter us, to keep us warm in winter and cool in summer, but to relax us, to dignify us, to encompass us with soft music and interesting hobbies, to be a playground, a theatre, and a bar. We expect our two-week vacation to be romantic, exotic, cheap and effortless. We expect a far-away atmosphere if we go to a near-by place; and we expect everything to be relaxing, sanitary, and Americanized if we go to a far-away place. We expect new heroes every season, a literary masterpiece every month, a dramatic spectacular every week, a rare sensation every night. We expect everybody to feel free to disagree, yet we expect everybody to be loyal, not to rock the boat or take the Fifth Amendment. We expect everybody to believe deeply in his religion, yet not to think less of others for not believing. We expect our nation to be strong and great and vast and varied and prepared for every challenge; yet we expect our "national purpose" to be clear and simple, something that

Big Nanny Is Watching

gives direction to the lives of two hundred million people and yet can be bought in a paperback at the corner drugstore for a dollar.

We expect anything and everything. We expect the contradictory and the impossible. We expect compact cars which are spacious; luxurious cars which are economical. We expect to be rich and charitable, powerful and merciful, active and reflective, kind and competitive. We expect to be inspired by mediocre appeals for "excellence," to be made literate by illiterate appeals for literacy. We expect to eat and stay thin, to be constantly on the move and ever more neighbourly, to go to the "church of our choice" and yet feel its guiding power over us, to revere God and to be God.

Never have people been more the masters of their environment. Yet never has a people felt more deceived and disappointed.

Ah, Brave New World! Boorstin neglected to mention that the word *culture*, as in "modern culture," also refers to something grown in an artificial medium. For instance, a virus.

PART FIVE

Finding GOD in the Cracks

CHAPTER 29

Five Polluted Words

One day my wife, Janet, who was directing a senior citizens' program in one of Chicago's poorest neighborhoods, came across this quote: "The poor express their gratitude not by saying thanks but by asking for more." She had just spent an exhausting day, and felt besieged by whiny, insistent demands for ever more help. That quote proved strangely comforting, she told me.

Why is it that the poor express their gratitude so indirectly? I wondered. Why don't they simply give thanks? After talking with Janet about her many experiences on the job, I concluded it is because of shame—shame over their need for help in the first place. I know how hard it is for me to ask someone else for help. What would it be like to live in a constant state of neediness?

More to the point, how can those of us who give to others do so without somehow undermining their sense of dignity? Due to my writer's instinct, I immediately started thinking of individual words, and I began to make a list of these words. All of them began as a pure expression of *giving* but became polluted over time. Such words litter the English language; taken together, they offer a strong warning about the dangers inherent in giving and receiving.

Pity. Deriving from the same root as *piety* and *pious*, this word once denoted a high form of sacrificial love. God, a perfect Being without needs, nevertheless chose to give of himself to his creatures. God had pity on needy people, such as the Israelite slaves in Egypt. God's ultimate act of self-giving, the Incarnation, can actually be seen as an act of pity, motivated out of God's love for us fallen human creatures. On earth, Jesus often felt moved with compassion, or pity. Those who mimicked him—the rich having "pity" on the poor, for example—thus expressed Godlike qualities.

That was the older meaning of the word, at least. Eventually, emphasis shifted from the givers of pity to the recipients, who were seen as weak and inferior. Now we hear the taunt, "I don't want your pity!" One who shows pity is condescending, even *un*loving—the meaning of the word has nearly inverted.

Charity. The IRS still recognizes the inherent goodness of this word—the agency grants tax exemptions to "charitable" organizations—but surely it, too, has lost some luster. In the Bible's King James Version of 1611, 1 Corinthians 13 renders *charity* as a direct translation of *agape*, the most exalted form of love, the kind of love that most nearly resembles God's love. Charity flows from a person who is patient, kind, forgiving, humble; charity never fails to discern the best in people.

158

Yet once again the meaning inverted over time: now no one wants to be a charity case. We accept charity only in desperation, as a last resort.

Condescend. I view the entire Bible as a step-by-step history of God's con-descensions. To Adam in the garden, to Moses in the burning bush, to the Israelites in the glory cloud, and finally to all of us in the Incarnation, he con- (meaning *with*) descended, or "descended to be with" us. A true Christian follows that example, as the apostle Paul clearly outlined in this passage: "Your attitude should be the same as that of Christ Jesus: Who, being in very nature God, did not consider equality with God something to be grasped, but made himself nothing, taking the very nature of a servant, being made in human likeness" (Philippians 2:5–7).

Once again, though, over time the word's meaning leaked away. We have lost the fine art of condescension. Who of us would welcome the remark, "You're so condescending!"?

Patronize. I have a special fondness for this word, for artists, musicians, and, yes, writers were once relieved of everyday anxieties about earning a living due to the generosity of *patrons*. Nowadays, however, there are few patrons, and fewer still who would want to be called patronizing. The *Random House Webster's Dictionary* defines *patronize* as "to behave in an offensively *condescending* manner toward"!

Paternalism. Another fine word, badly tainted. The root comes from *pater*, or "father." In older days, a paternalistic person reminded others of a kindly father who cared for the needs of his children; now the image more resembles an insensitive stepfather who reeks of superiority as he stoops down to help his charges.

> Perhaps an ancient Chinese proverb expresses the problem best: "Nothing atones for the insult of a gift but the love of the giver."

Why have these words changed in meaning? Each of them, once honorable and majestic, gradually melted like a wax statue into a sad lump barely resembling its former self. The words have changed, quite simply, because we humans have failed so often and so badly at the difficult task of giving. Perhaps an ancient Chinese proverb expresses the problem best: "Nothing atones for the insult of a gift but the love of the giver."

A Christian organization carrying out relief work in a needy country, my wife as she ministers one-on-one to senior citizens or the homeless, I as I confront a beggar on the street—each of us confronts the vast and perilous gap between the giver and the receiver. Government programs established with the highest of motives often founder for reasons that can be glimpsed in these polluted words. An institution cannot love; only people can love. As the proverb says, apart from love, giving becomes an insult.

We could all avoid these problems if we simply ignored the needy and associated with self-sufficient people exclusively. However, reaching out to the needy is not an option for the Christian. It is a command. I wrote a book entitled *Where Is God When It Hurts?* The real answer to that question, the answer implicit in the New Testament, is another question: Where is the church when it hurts? We followers of Jesus are God's primary response to the massive needs of the world. We are literally Christ's body.

When Jesus lived here in a physical body, he spent time among the poor, the widowed, the paralyzed, and even those with dreaded diseases. People with leprosy, for example—the AIDS patients of ancient times—were required to cry out, "Unclean! Unclean!" if anyone approached; touching such a person went against the laws of Moses. Yet Jesus defied law and custom by going up to leprosy patients and touching them—an act of astonishing condescension. That has been God's consistent pattern in all of history.

We in the church, God's body on earth, are likewise called to move toward those who suffer. We are, after all, God's means of expressing his love to the world, which is why words such as *pity* and *charity* originated as religious words.

Can we reclaim these polluted words—or, if not the words, then at least the meaning behind them? I take some hope in the fact that all the words in the above list retain at least a glimmer of their theological origin. There is a way to make pity Godlike; charity can convey a high form of love; condescension may lead to unity, not division; a patron may exalt, not demean, his subjects; paternalism may, in fact, remind us of our true state as children of a heavenly Father.

Indeed, I know of only one way to eliminate the great gap between giver and receiver, and that is a humble recognition that all of us are needy beggars, sustained each moment by the mercy of a sovereign God. Only as we experience God's grace as pure grace, not something we earned or worked for, can we offer love with no strings attached to another person in need. There is but one true Giver in the universe; all else are debtors.

CHAPTER 30

The Peculiar Advantages of Poverty

Jesus and Karl Marx have at least one thing in common: a paradoxical view of poverty. Both tend to (1) exalt the poor, but (2) devote energies to making everyone "unpoor."

The second part of that formula I readily understand. Having grown up in circumstances well below the official poverty line, I now support efforts to provide jobs, housing, medical care, and basic human services for people who lack them. But what about the first part? "Blessed are the poor," Jesus said bluntly. The people I grew up around seemed no more virtuous or admirable than anyone else. Indeed, most of us yearned to escape poverty. Why, then, should they be called blessed?

The phrase "God's preferential option for the poor" has only increased my puzzlement. Why would God single out the poor for special attention over any other group? I do not contest the phrase; the Catholic bishops who first adopted it assembled an impressive list of supportive passages from the Old and New Testaments. One need only read through the Beatitudes (the section of statements in the Gospels that begin "Blessed are . . .") to gain a sense of Jesus' favoritism toward the poor and the disadvantaged. My question is, Why? What makes the poor deserving of God's concern?

This paradox in the Beatitudes has long puzzled me, and as I reflect back, I can see that my understanding of them has gone through three stages.

1. Dangled Promises. I once viewed the Beatitudes as a kind of sop Jesus threw to the unfortunates. "Well, since you aren't rich, and your health is bad, and your face is wet with tears, I'll toss out a few nice phrases to make you feel better."

Unlike medieval kings who threw coins to the masses (or modern politicians who rant about the poor and homeless just before elections), though, Jesus had the advantage of dangling before his audience real rewards. He who came down from heaven knew well that the spoils of the kingdom of heaven would easily counterbalance whatever misery we might encounter here on earth.

Among many Christians, an emphasis on future rewards has gone out of fashion. My former pastor Bill Leslie used to observe, "As churches grow wealthier and more successful, they're less likely to sing 'This world is not my home, I'm just a passin' through' and more likely to intone 'This is my father's world.' " Perhaps we Christians, in the U.S. anyway, have grown so comfortable that we no longer identify with the earthly conditions Jesus addressed in the Beatitudes, which helps explain why they sound so strange to us.

Yet we dare not discount the value of hope in future rewards. One need only listen to the songs composed by American slaves to realize this consolation of belief. "Swing low, sweet chariot, comin' for to carry me home." "When I get to heaven, goin' to put on my robe, goin' to shout all over God's heaven." "Nobody knows the trouble I've seen, nobody knows but Jesus."

Over time I have learned to respect, and even long for, the future rewards Jesus promised. Even so, these rewards lay somewhere in the future. Dangled promises do not always satisfy immediate needs.

2. The Great Reversal. The Beatitudes describe the present as well as the future, neatly contrasting how to succeed in the "kingdom of heaven" versus the "kingdom of this world."

Visit a magazine rack in any drugstore and you will see a vivid display of the values honored in this world. *Fortune, Money, Travel and*

Leisure, and their clones extol the advantages of wealth and economic success. *Cosmopolitan, Esquire, Body Builder, Swimsuit*, and several rows of soft-porn titles flaunt our obsession with image and physical appearance. Then come the racks of true crime stories, Gothic romances, and soap opera digests that satisfy our society's thirst for unrighteousness.

The Beatitudes express quite plainly that God views this world with different lenses. Strength, good looks, connections, and the competitive instinct may bring a person success in a society like ours; but those very qualities may block entrance to the kingdom of heaven. Dependence, sorrow, repentance—these are the steps to God's kingdom.

> One need only read through the Beatitudes to gain a sense of Jesus' favoritism toward the poor and the disadvantaged. My question is, Why?

I do not believe the poor to be more virtuous than anyone else, but they are less likely to pretend to be virtuous. As an example, consider the single word *dependence*. Workaholics and status-seekers may spend half their lives trying to disprove their need to depend on anyone else, including God. But we are *creatures*, dependent by nature, and a repressed dependence will leak out, often in the form of addiction. It is no accident that twelve-step groups modeled after Alcoholics Anonymous require each struggler to begin by admitting a dependence on other people and on a "higher power." Meanwhile, the poor never have the luxury of repressing their needs; they depend on others simply to survive.

People who are rich, successful, and beautiful may go through life relying on their natural gifts. But there's a chance, just a chance, that people who lack such natural advantages may cry out to God in their time of need. Through no choice of their own—they may urgently wish otherwise—poor people find themselves in a posture that befits the grace of

God. They are needy, dependent, and dissatisfied with life; for that reason they may welcome God's free gift of love. We need the poor to teach us the value of dependence, for unless we learn dependence we will never experience grace.

The Beatitudes reveal at once God's "preferential option for the poor" and the poor's "preferential option for God." Underqualified for success in the kingdom of this world, they just may turn to God. "Blessed are the *desperate*" is how one commentator translates "poor in spirit." Human beings do not readily admit desperation. When they do, the kingdom of heaven draws near.

3. Psychological Reality. More recently, I have come to see a third level of truth in the Beatitudes. A book like Paul Johnson's *Intellectuals* sets out in convincing detail what all of us know to be true: the people we laud, strive to emulate, and feature on the covers of those drugstore magazines are not the fulfilled, happy, balanced persons we might imagine. Although Johnson's subjects (Ernest Hemingway, Bertrand Russell, Jean-Paul Sartre, Edmund Wilson, Bertolt Brecht, et al.) would be judged successful by any modern standard, it would be difficult to assemble a more miserable, egomaniacal, abusive company.

True greatness, paradoxical as it may seem, grows from different soil. As I look back over the people in my own life who have manifested the greatest wisdom, they include the following: a patient at a leprosarium in India; a civil rights worker who worked out his theology in a jail cell; a mother who lost two children to cystic fibrosis; a priest who took a vow of chastity, poverty, and obedience, and now works at a home for the severely disabled; a minister-turned-innkeeper who runs a hotel for the homeless.

I am beginning, I think, to understand the Beatitudes at last. I now view them not as patronizing slogans, but as profound insights into the mystery of human existence. The poor, the hungry, the mourners, and the oppressed really are blessed. Not because of their miserable states, of course—Jesus spent much of his life trying to remedy those miseries.

Rather, they are blessed because of an innate advantage they hold over those more comfortable and self-sufficient.

The Beatitudes still jar me every time I read them, but they jar me because I now recognize in them a richness that unmasks my own poverty.

CHAPTER 31

Miracle on LaSalle Street

I first met Bill Leslie in a grungy pizza parlor after a DePaul University basketball game. I was surprised to find an overweight white man who dressed carelessly, talked too loud, and laughed uproariously at his own jokes. This was the minister of Chicago's renowned LaSalle Street Church?

Out of curiosity I attended LaSalle the following Sunday, and ended up staying there for thirteen years. I got to know Bill well, especially after my wife accepted a job directing one of the church's outreach programs. Bill talked too loud in the pulpit, too, and laughed at his own oft-repeated jokes, and occasionally slaughtered the English language. But he became our pastor, and we grew to love him, and when he died unexpectedly of a heart attack at the age of sixty, Janet and I joined many other Chicagoans in grieving the loss.

Bill Leslie served the same church for twenty-eight years, and what a time it was. The congregation met in a building whose walls can tell the history of Chicago: German-speaking Lutherans laid the cornerstone in 1882, and Italians, Japanese, and Appalachian whites all took turns in the building until hippies and then yuppies moved in. When Bill became pastor in 1961, the church stood midway between the richest and poorest communities of Chicago. Two blocks to the east lay the Gold Coast, average income over $50,000; two blocks to the west lay the Cabrini-Green housing project, average income under $3,000. While studying the biblical prophets' words on justice, LaSalle caught a vision of being a "bridge church" between the two neighborhoods.

After several years of commuting from the comfortable suburb of Wheaton, Bill Leslie heard God's call to join the neighborhood. It was 1968, the worst time possible for such a move. After Martin Luther King, Jr.'s assassination, angry blacks burned down thirty square blocks of buildings; the church stuck out amid the rubble, preserved because of its good reputation in the community. National Guardsmen patrolled the streets. The Leslies could find no one willing to insure their urban home.

A few years later, three men attacked Bill in the sanctuary, hoping to steal the morning offering. They hit him on the head with a bowling pin, stomped on his groin, and battered him with a fire extinguisher. Stripped of clothing, gagged, hogtied, Bill lay in the vestibule and reconsidered his call to the city.

But he did not give up. Too much was happening in the fledgling congregation for him to walk away. Neighborhood outreach started when Sunday school teachers, noticing that many students could not read, offered tutoring classes after the Sunday service. The need was enormous—the local high school had a dropout rate of 75 percent. Soon busloads of students from nearby evangelical Wheaton College were making their way to LaSalle Street to help with one-on-one tutoring.

Since unemployment among the working-age population of Cabrini averaged 86 percent, most kids from the projects hung out on street corners all day. During summer months, someone in the neighborhood is shot an average of once every other day. Bill and others at the church saw a need for recreational programs. They bought a pool table, set up a basketball court, and raised money for football equipment (the high school team, with only thirteen helmets, was scrimmaging with seven players lined up on offense and six on defense). Before long an urban Young Life program had sprung up, affiliated with the church.

More needs surfaced. When a government study reported that a third of all dog and cat food was bought by senior citizens too poor to afford "people food," the church began a ministry to local seniors. To counter neighborhood abuse by the police and by landlords, an attorney quit his firm to begin a Legal Aid Clinic, offering free legal representation to any Cabrini-Green resident with qualifying income. A counseling center was established, with sliding fees based on income.

> Stripped of clothing, gagged, hogtied, Bill lay in the vestibule and reconsidered his call to the city.

In Chicago, as in most cities, half of all babies are born to single mothers, and soon the church founded a ministry to assist them as well. Bill was most proud, however, of a housing project that he first dreamed of when the church's annual budget was $20,000. Somehow, with LaSalle leading the way to secure grants and loans, the $11 million development became a reality. Economically and racially mixed, Atrium Village is credited with anchoring the community and reversing neighborhood decay.

169

Bill Leslie was a most unlikely pioneer. He was disheveled, disorganized (several times I waited in vain for Bill, who had forgotten our appointment or gone to the wrong restaurant), and hardly a promising candidate for racial reconciliation (he had been student body president at the strictly segregated Bob Jones University, and his father-in-law had worked in racist Lester Maddox's gubernatorial campaign). Yet he, as much as anyone, was responsible for pointing the evangelical church back to the city, and for reminding us that Jesus came to redeem communities as well as individual souls. He helped found a program to train young seminarians in urban ministry. Now, in many U.S. cities, young Christians are moving in as pioneers to lead the way in community development.

Three decades in the inner city took a toll on Bill and his family. He never did learn to say no. At the memorial service, one woman glowingly recalled that Bill had spent eight hours counseling her the day before he departed on a month-long trip to Greece. A member of the congregation acknowledged the other side, addressing the Leslie family directly: "I'm sorry that Bill gave us so much and had so little left over for you."

Bill Leslie did some things wrong, but he got one thing right: he understood the grace of God. Grace became the church's theme: its fifty-year anniversary banquet featured a large banner that read, "This far by grace."

Bill Leslie recognized his own endless need for grace, preached it almost every Sunday, and offered it to everyone around him in starkly practical ways. Because of his faithfulness, the near-north side of Chicago is a very different place today. And so, I believe, is heaven.

Yvonne Delk, a powerful black woman who leads the Community Renewal Society, summed up Bill's life with simple eloquence, "He was biblical without being fundamentalist, spiritual without being withdrawn from the world, and actively engaged with the world but not conformed to it. You have fought the good fight, Bill, you have finished the course, you have kept the faith. We are grateful for a man sent from God to Chicago whose name is Bill."

The Surprise of Faith

The Gospels normally use the miracles to stress Jesus' power and authority. At least nine stories, however, focus on *faith*. "Your faith has healed you," Jesus would say, shifting attention from himself to the healed person. Miraculous power did not come from his side alone; sometimes it somehow depended on an individual's response.

I once read through all the miracle stories together and found they reveal remarkably different degrees of faith. A few people demonstrated bold, unshakable faith, such as a centurion who told Jesus he need not bother with a visit—just a word would heal his servant long-distance. "I tell you the truth, I have not found anyone in Israel with such great faith," Jesus remarked, astonished.

Another time, a foreign woman pursued Jesus as he was seeking peace and quiet. At first Jesus answered her not a word. Then he replied sharply, telling her he was sent to the lost sheep of Israel, not to "dogs"—referring to her status as a Gentile. But nothing could deter this Canaanite woman, and her perseverance won Jesus over. "Woman, you have great faith!" he said.

Jesus seemed impressed that, as foreigners, these were the *least likely* people to demonstrate great faith. Why should a centurion and a Canaanite, who had no Jewish roots, put their trust in a Messiah his own countrymen had trouble accepting?

These stories threaten me, because seldom do I have such outstanding faith. Unlike the Canaanite woman, I am easily discouraged by the silence of God. When my prayers do not seem to be answered, I am tempted to give up, and not ask again. I identify more readily with the wavering man who declared to Jesus, "I do believe; help me overcome my unbelief!" All too often I find myself echoing those words, dangling somewhere between belief and unbelief, wondering how much I miss out on by my lack of faith.

Sometimes, Jesus was amazed by the lack of faith he came across. Mark gives this extraordinary comment about Jesus' visit to his hometown: "He could not do any miracles there, except lay his hands on a few sick people and heal them." In a strange way, God's power was "paralyzed" by a lack of faith.

To my surprise, I noticed as I read through the stories that the people who knew Jesus best sometimes faltered in their faith. It was his own neighbors who doubted him. John the Baptist, who had proclaimed, "Look, the Lamb of God!" and had heard a voice from heaven at Jesus' baptism, later questioned him. And several times Jesus remarked with astonishment on the twelve disciples' faithlessness.

Jesus' three most intimate disciples saw a dramatic miracle shortly before his death. On the Mount of Transfiguration, Jesus' face shone like the sun, and his clothes became dazzling white. A cloud enveloped the disciples, and inside that cloud, to their astonishment, they found two long-dead giants of Jewish history: Moses and Elijah. It was too much for the dazed disciples to take in; when God spoke audibly in the cloud, they fell down, terror-stricken. Yet what impact did such a stupendous event have? Shortly, the eyewitnesses of the Transfiguration joined the rest of the Twelve in abandoning—*denying*, in Peter's case—Jesus in his hour of deepest need.

We easily forget that Judas had for three years watched Jesus work great miracles and listened to his teaching; even so, he betrayed Jesus. Another disciple, "doubting Thomas," gained the reputation as a skeptic, but in truth all the disciples showed a lack of faith. None of them believed the wild reports the women brought back from the empty tomb. Even after Jesus appeared to them in person, says Matthew, "some doubted."

A curious law of reversal seems to be at work in the Gospels: Faith appears where least expected and falters where it should be thriving.

I remember my first visit to Old Faithful in Yellowstone National Park. Rings of Japanese and German tourists surrounded the geyser, their video cameras trained like weapons on the famous hole in the ground. A large digital clock stood beside the spot, predicting twenty-four minutes until the next eruption.

> All too often I find
> myself dangling
> somewhere between
> belief and unbelief,
> wondering how much
> I miss out on by
> my lack of faith.

My wife and I passed the countdown in the dining room of Old Faithful Inn overlooking the geyser. When the digital clock reached one minute, we along with every other diner left our seats and rushed to the windows to see the big wet event.

I noticed that immediately, as if on signal, a crew of busboys and waiters descended on the tables to refill water glasses and clear away dirty dishes. When the geyser went off, we tourists oohed and aahed and clicked our cameras; a few spontaneously applauded. But, glancing back over my shoulder, I saw that not a single waiter or busboy—not even those who had finished their chores—looked out the huge windows. Old Faithful, grown entirely too familiar, had lost its power to impress them.

A little later, our church back in Chicago faced something of a crisis. The pastor had left, attendance was flagging, a community outreach program now seemed threatened. The leadership suggested an all-night vigil of prayer.

Several people raised questions. Was it safe, given our inner-city neighborhood? Should we hire guards or escorts for the parking lot? What if no one showed up? At length we discussed the logistics and the "practicality" of such an event. Nevertheless, the night of prayer was scheduled.

To my surprise the poorest members of the congregation, a group of senior citizens from a housing project, were the ones who responded most enthusiastically to the prayer vigil. I could not help wondering how many of their prayers had gone unanswered over the years—they lived in the projects, after all, amid crime, poverty, and suffering—yet still they showed a childlike trust in the power of prayer. "How long do you want to stay—an hour or two?" we asked, thinking of the logistics of van shuttles. "Oh, we'll stay all night," they replied.

One black woman in her nineties, who walks with a cane and can barely see, explained to a staff member why she wanted to spend the night sitting on the hard pews of a church in an unsafe neighborhood. "You see, they's lots of things we can't do in this church. We ain't so educated, and we ain't got as much energy as some of you younger folks. But we can pray. We got time, and we got faith. Some of us don't sleep much anyway. We can pray all night if needs be."

And so they did. Meanwhile, a bunch of yuppies in a downtown church learned anew a lesson of faith from the Gospels: Faith appears where least expected and falters where it should be thriving.

CHAPTER 33

The Alchemy of Memory

One Christmas I got into an extended conversation with my grandmother, who was born in 1898. "Who was your favorite president?" I asked. She thought for a moment and replied, "Roosevelt."

"I can understand that," I replied. "After all, he led us during World War II, and started many important programs, like Social Security."

"Oh, no," she interrupted. "I mean Teddy Roosevelt. Now there was a real man!"

Later, when I was discussing my visit to Russia to witness the fall of Communism, my grandmother piped in, "Oh, yes, I remember when the Communists first took over [in 1917]. That was scary." Being older than the century gives one a certain perspective: she had watched the full cycle as a powerful ideology appeared on the scene, burst into light, then faded away like a dying star.

As I probed my grandmother's astonishing memory, I noticed a trend that seems almost universal in the reminiscences of older people: they tend to recall difficult, tumultuous times with a touch of nostalgia. According to polls, 60 percent of Londoners who survived the Blitz now remember that time as the happiest period of their lives. Somehow a new spirit of community and patriotism sprang up to eclipse even the horror of bombs and V-2 rockets. In the United States, the elderly swap stories about World War II and the Great Depression; they speak fondly of hardships such as blizzards, the childhood outhouse, and the time in college when they ate canned soup and stale bread three weeks in a row.

I ran into this pattern again when I worked on the memoirs *(Pain: The Gift Nobody Wants)* of Dr. Paul Brand, a missionary surgeon who has entered his ninth decade of life and sixth decade of marriage. As I interviewed him and his wife, Margaret, about their life together, they, too, kept circling back to the crisis moments.

For example, there was the interval in 1946–47 when Paul had preceded Margaret to Vellore, India. In that year of independence and partition, unrest between Hindus and Muslims began spreading across the northern part of the country. In southern India, though, especially the region around Vellore, Hindus and Muslims lived together in reasonable harmony. Thus Paul wrote and asked his young wife to bring their two infant children and join him as soon as possible.

Back in England, things did not look so rosy. London papers reported that violence was sweeping across India, forcing the greatest human migration in history. Four million refugees had fled to the city of Calcutta alone. In the northwest, Sikhs boarded trains, made men pull down their pants, and killed all those circumcised (Muslims); Pakistanis waylaid trains going the opposite direction and killed the uncircumcised (Hindus).

Paul Brand's glowing reports of the situation in Vellore contradicted the frightening headlines Margaret was reading in London: "SLAUGHTER IN THE PUNJAB. . . . BRINK OF CIVIL WAR. . . . MASSACRE OF EUROPEANS PREDICTED." Her family, not realizing the nearest trouble spots were a thousand miles from Vellore, thought it the height of folly for her to take two babies to such a place. But Margaret, trusting her husband, took a leap of faith and did so.

There were other family crises as well, and I have heard versions from both Paul and Margaret. At the time, these dramatic intrusions seemed to call into question their entire relationship. But now they retell the stories with nostalgia, for the crises fit together into—indeed, helped form—a pattern of love and trust. Looking back, from the vantage point of fifty years, it seems clear that the Brands' mutual response to the stormy times was what gave their marriage its enduring strength.

Every marriage has crisis times, moments of truth when one partner (or both) is tempted to give up, to judge the other undependable, irrational, untrustworthy. Great marriages survive these moments; weak ones fall apart. When divorce happens, tragically, both partners lose out on the deeper strength that comes only from riding out such stormy times together. If, for example, Margaret Brand had judged her husband crazy for beckoning her to India

> Partly from listening to elderly people, I have learned that faith means trusting in advance what will only make sense in reverse.

in the midst of political turmoil, and filed for divorce—how sad that would have been. A splendid marriage and partnership in God's work would have been irretrievably lost.

177

Great relationships take form when they are stretched to the breaking point and do not break. Seeing this principle lived out in people like the Brands, I can better understand one of the mysteries of relating to God. Abraham climbing the hill at Moriah, Job scratching his boils in the hot sun, David hiding in a cave, Elijah moping in a desert, Moses pleading for a new job description—all these heroes experienced crisis moments when they were sorely tempted to judge God uncaring, powerless, or even malign. Confused and in the dark, they faced a turning point: whether to turn away embittered, or step forward in faith. In the end, all chose the path of trust, and for this reason we remember them as giants of faith.

The Bible is littered with tales of others—Cain, Samson, Solomon, Judas—who flunked such tests. Their lives, like the marriages that fail too soon, give off a scent of sadness and remorse: Oh, what might have been.

In America, I've noticed, a consumer mentality tends to infiltrate relationships as well as commerce. Some people treat marriage partners like automobiles; every few years it's time to upgrade to a new model. Some Christians treat churches the same way. And some even approach God with a consumer spirit: when God performs satisfactorily, he merits our worship, but when God seems distant or unresponsive, why bother?

Why bother? Because the deepest strength only comes through testing.

Partly from listening to elderly people, I have learned that faith means trusting in advance what will only make sense in reverse. Fifty years casts another light on marriage; the century looks different from a grandmother's view. And I believe that human history will take on a new look from the vantage point of eternity. Every scar, every hurt, every disappointment will be seen in a different light, bathed in an eternity of love and trust. Not even the murder of God's own Son could end the relationship between God and human beings. In the alchemy of redemption, that most villainous crime became a day we now call Good Friday.

CHAPTER 34

Will God Forgive What I'm About to Do?

S teven Spielberg's film version of *The Color Purple* includes a moving portrayal of a parable of grace. Sugar, a sexy, knock-'em-dead nightclub singer who works out of a ramshackle bar by the side of a river, is the classic prodigal daughter. Her father, a minister who preaches hellfire and brimstone in a church just across the way, hasn't spoken to her in years.

One day as Sug is crooning "I've got somethin' to tell you" in the bar, she hears the church choir answer, as if antiphonally, "God's got something to tell you!" Pricked by nostalgia or guilt, Sug leads her band to the church and marches down the aisle just as her father mounts the pulpit to preach on the prodigal son.

The sight of his long-lost daughter silences the minister, and he glowers at the procession coming down the aisle. "Even us sinners have soul," Sug explains, and hugs her father, who hardly reacts. Ever the moralist, he cannot easily forgive a daughter who has shamed him so.

The Hollywood portrayal, however, altogether misses the main point of the biblical parable. In Jesus' version the father does not glower, but rather searches the horizon, desperate for any sign of his wayward

179

child. It is the father who runs, throws his arm around the prodigal, and kisses him.

By making a sinner the magnanimous hero, Hollywood dodges the scandal of grace. In truth what blocks forgiveness is not God's reticence—"But while he was still a long way off, his father saw him and was filled with compassion for him"—but ours. God's arms are always extended; we are the ones who turn away. It is a wonderful truth, and one subject to devious exploitation.

Not long ago I sat in a restaurant and listened to yet another variation on a familiar theme. Daniel confided that he had decided to leave his wife after fifteen years of marriage. He had met someone younger and prettier, he said, someone who "makes me feel alive, like I haven't felt in years."

Daniel, a Christian, knew well the personal and moral consequences of what he was about to do. His decision to leave would inflict permanent damage on his wife and three children. Even so, he said, the force pulling him toward the younger woman was too strong to resist.

I listened to his story with sadness and grief. Then, during the dessert course, he dropped the bombshell, "The reason I wanted to see you tonight was to ask you a question. Do you think God can forgive something as awful as I am about to do?"

Historian and art critic Robert Hughes tells of a convict sentenced to life imprisonment on a maximum security island off the coast of Australia. One day with no provocation he turned on a fellow prisoner he barely knew and beat him senseless. The murderer was shipped back to the mainland to stand trial, where he gave a straightforward, passionless account of the crime, showing no sign of remorse. "Why?" asked the bewildered judge. "What was your motive?"

The prisoner replied that he was sick of life on the island, a notoriously brutal place, and that he saw no reason to keep on living. "Yes, yes,

I understand all that," said the judge. "I can see why you might drown yourself in the ocean. But why murder?"

"Well, it's like this," said the prisoner. "I'm a Catholic. If I commit suicide I'll go straight to hell. But if I murder I can come back here and confess to a priest before my execution. That way, God will forgive me."

Do we fully appreciate the *scandal* of unconditional grace? How can I dissuade my friend Daniel from committing a terrible mistake if he knows forgiveness lies just around the corner? Or, worse, why not murder, like the Australian prisoner, if you know in advance you'll be forgiven?

> Daniel confided that he had decided to leave his wife after fifteen years of marriage.

The scandal of grace must have haunted the apostle Paul as he wrote the book of Romans. The first three chapters ring down condemnation on every class of human being, concluding, "There is no one righteous, not even one." The next two chapters unveil the miracle of a grace so boundless that, as Paul says, "where sin increased, grace increased all the more."

Paul's tone changes in chapter 6. I can almost see the apostle staring at the papyrus and scratching his head, thinking to himself, *Wait a minute! What have I said?* What's to keep a murderer, adulterer, or common sinner from exploiting God's lavish promise of "forgiveness in advance"?

More than once in the next few chapters Paul returns to this logical predicament: "What shall we say, then? Shall we go on sinning so that grace may increase?" To such a devious question he has a pithy answer ("By no means!" or, as the King James Version has it, "God forbid!") and a lengthy one. What Paul keeps circling around in those dense, wonderful chapters (6–8) is, quite simply, the scandal of grace.

Will God Forgive What I'm About to Do?

* * *

Here is what I told my friend Daniel, in a nutshell. "Can God forgive you? Of course. Read your Bible. David, Peter, Paul—God builds his church on the backs of people who murder, commit adultery, deny him, and persecute his followers. But because of Christ, forgiveness is now our problem, not God's. What we have to go through to commit sin distances us from God—we change in the very act of rebellion—and there is no guarantee we will come back. You ask me about forgiveness now, but will you even want it later, especially if it involves repentance?"

Several months after our conversation, Daniel made his choice. I have yet to see any evidence of repentance. Now he tends to rationalize his decision as a way of escaping an unhappy marriage. He has rejected most of his Christian friends—"Too narrow-minded," he says—and looks instead for people who celebrate his newfound liberation.

To me, though, Daniel does not seem very liberated. The price of his "freedom" has meant turning his back on those who cared about him most. He also tells me God is not a part of his life right now. "Maybe later," he says.

God took a great risk by announcing forgiveness in advance. It occurs to me, though, that the scandal of grace involves a transfer of that risk to us. As George MacDonald put it, we are condemned not for the wicked things we've done, but for not leaving them.

FINDING GOD in Unexpected PLACES

CHAPTER 35

Holy Secrets

Almost everyone has occasion to wish for an ability to see into the future. *Is this person the one I should marry? Should I accept that new job offer? How will my rebellious son turn out? If only, dear God, I could have a glimpse of the future, a mere clue as to how it will turn out, decisions would be so much simpler.*

What would Abraham Lincoln or Winston Churchill have given for such preternatural vision during their crises of war? What would the CIA pay for certain knowledge of how Eastern Europe will look ten years from now?

As I read the Bible, though, I can begin to understand why God seldom shares inside information about the future. The plain fact is, most human beings cannot handle it.

Take the prophet Balaam, a mysterious Old Testament character who received a series of unmistakable messages from God about the Israelites' future (although it required a talking donkey to overcome his initial resistance). In the end, Balaam failed to heed his own message, working against the very Israelites whose triumph he had predicted. He was finally executed as an enemy of God's people. (See Numbers 22–24; 31; Deuteronomy 23.)

Or consider Hezekiah. One of Judah's best kings, he received from God an unprecedented extension to his life. But once he learned of those fifteen bonus years, Hezekiah set about squandering them; in the process he sowed the seeds for his nation's downfall and eventual captivity by Babylon. (See 2 Kings 18–20; 2 Chronicles 29–32; Isaiah 39.)

The classic Old Testament tale of foreknowledge centers on Saul and David. The prophet Samuel delivered a similar announcement to both of them: Saul would lose the kingdom, for God had chosen another to lead the nation. King Saul spent the next decade or so in rebellion against that future, trying desperately to kill the one whom God had designated as his replacement. David, who shared the same foreknowledge, makes a striking contrast. Refusing to take the future into his own hands, he turned down several chances to depose Saul, and as a result spent those years hiding out in caves and deserts. The Psalms reveal that he sometimes wondered whether God had forgotten about the plan, but even so David remained faithful. (See 1 Samuel 9–31.)

In the New Testament, the apostle Paul offers another example of the wise use of foreknowledge. Bad news about the future didn't scare him: he traveled to Jerusalem despite strong warnings that a visit would result in his arrest and imprisonment. But good news about the future didn't make him cocky or passive: after learning in a vision that all passengers would survive a shipwreck off Malta, Paul took command, giving instructions to the Roman guards and mobilizing the rescue efforts. (See Acts 20–21; 27–28.)

These and many other biblical examples make clear that human beings don't easily cope with advance knowledge of the future. (Adam and Eve certainly didn't.) They are far more likely to respond by either rebelling against bad news, as King Saul and Balaam did, or getting cocky about good news, as Hezekiah did.

I once viewed foreknowledge as a "genie in a bottle" gift of magic that affords the recipient an enviable advantage. I now see it as a rather demanding test of faith. David in exile dreaming of his coronation, Hezekiah debating fifteen-year plans, the apostle Paul riding out a Mediterranean storm, even Jesus praying in Gethsemane—all had special foresight into what end awaited them, but that hardly made the *process* any easier. It takes an extra measure of faith to endure with patience and obedience the long hours or years that precede whatever future you know about in advance. Ask the Old Testament prophets.

*   *   *

Unlike Balaam, Hezekiah, Saul, and David, most of us today do not receive a special revelation as to how our specific future will turn out. (Frankly, as I look back on their lives, I'm glad.) But in at least one instance all Christians face a test of "responsible foreknowledge." It involves the spectacular good news about God's grace and forgiveness as revealed in Jesus' parables and in such New Testament letters as Romans and Galatians.

> If a bridegroom on his wedding night sat down to negotiate terms of infidelity, we would call such a husband a fraud.

"Therefore, there is now no condemnation for those who are in Christ Jesus," Paul proclaims in Romans 8. That's about as sweeping a statement as he could make—and far more dangerous than if he had said, "Well, God can't promise anything. There *may* not be any condemnation; it all depends on how you behave from now on." It seems that God the Judge has revealed his merciful verdict even before the trial begins!

Paul seems fully aware that advance knowledge of such all-encompassing good news might be subject to abuse. That is why in Romans 6, after proving that God's grace triumphs over all sin, he interrupts himself to ask the rhetorical question that captures the logic of someone intent on handling foreknowledge irresponsibly: "Shall we go on sinning so that grace may increase?" And why a few paragraphs later he stops again—like a preacher who realizes he's just said something outrageous—and rephrases the question.

The scandal of grace—God informing us of our forgiveness *in advance*—is probably the closest most of us will come to certain knowledge of the future. As my friend Daniel showed, that very knowledge opens up all sorts of devious possibilities.

More and more, I have begun to see that Paul's explosive response,

Holy Secrets

"God forbid!" is the only appropriate response to human questions about exploiting God's grace. If you're the kind of person who seizes upon God's grace just for the chance to push it to the limits, why, you probably haven't understood that grace at all.

If a bridegroom on his wedding night sat down to negotiate terms of infidelity—"OK, you've guaranteed the future by promising to stick with me regardless. Just how far can I go with other women? Can I hug them? Kiss them? Go to bed with them? How often? How many?"—we would call such a husband a fraud, a pathologically sick man. If he approaches marriage that way, he will never learn the meaning of true love. And if a Christian approaches forgiveness the same way—"Let's see, God has promised forgiveness in advance. What can I get away with? How far can I push it?"—that Christian will end up equally impoverished. Paul's response says it all: "God forbid!"

I have come to view God's grace as a matter of responsible fore-knowledge, not so different from the special revelations granted a few individuals in the Old and New Testaments. We know the future—God's forgiveness—and such advance knowledge presents us with a choice, a challenge of faith. We can set out to exploit God's promises by probing the outer limits of forgiveness. On the other hand, we can live in a spirit of gratitude, secure enough in his love to follow him faithfully. It was an extravagant risk God took, entrusting us with such holy secrets.

PART SIX

Finding GOD Within the Church

CHAPTER 36

The Church Behind Bars

I have always had a strange, intense curiosity about what happens when human beings are pressed to their limits. As a child, I used to read with quiet horror the stories in Foxe's *Book of Martyrs*. Anti-communism was a national sport in the 1950s, and preachers would regale us with tales of Christian martyrs in Russia and China and Albania. I even studied Chinese, and my brother Russian, to prepare for the day our country would surely be overrun. What would happen when my faith was tested to the extreme? Would I cling to Christ or renounce him to save my skin?

189

Perhaps because of these nagging questions, I took an unusual writing assignment a few years ago. A good friend, Ron Nikkel, invited me to visit some Christians in the prisons of Chile and Peru. South American jails, I knew, would provide an extreme test of faith for anyone. Although conditions have improved now, at the time Chile was viewed as one of the world's worst human rights violators. And Peruvian jails also make news headlines: hundreds of prisoners have died in riots there.

What does a "church" look like among lumpen people such as these: fenced in, ill-fed, vulnerable to sexual assaults, sentenced to years of misery among murderers, thieves, rapists, and drug dealers? Can the hope of the Christian message survive those conditions? I decided to find out.

I am sitting in the midst of a church service with a distinctly Latin and Pentecostal flavor. On the platform, a "band" consisting of eighteen guitarists, one accordionist, and two men wielding handmade brass tambourines is leading a rousing rendition of a folksy song called "The Banquet of the Lord."

The congregation, 150 strong, lustily joins in. Some people raise their hands above their heads. Some seem to be competing in a highest-decibel contest. A few hug their neighbors. The meeting room is overflowing, and extra faces are peering in all the windows.

Except for a few visual reminders, I could easily forget that we are meeting in one of the largest prisons in Chile. I look around at the congregation: all men, wearing a ragtag assortment of handed-down street clothes. A shocking number of their faces are marked with scars.

After the singing a Canadian guest, conspicuous in a white shirt and tie, comes to the platform. The prison chaplain informs the crowd that this man, Ron Nikkel, has visited prisons in more than fifty countries. The organization he directs, Prison Fellowship International, brings the message of Christ to prisoners and works with governments on improving prison conditions. A dozen inmates yell a loud "Amen!"

"I bring you greetings from your brothers and sisters in Christ in prisons around the world," Ron begins, pausing for the translation into Spanish. He is a broad-shouldered man of moderate height, with a freckled face that gives him a youthful look. His soft voice must compete with noise flowing in from the outside—guards blowing whistles, inmates playing basketball in the exercise yard, music blaring from the cell blocks.

"I bring you greetings especially from Pascal, who lives in Africa, in a country called Madagascar. Pascal trained as a scientist and took pride in his atheism. One day he was arrested for participating in a student strike. He was thrown into a prison designed for 800 men, but now crowded with 2,500 men. They sat elbow to elbow on bare boards, most of them dressed in rags and covered with lice. You can imagine the sanitation there." The Chilean inmates, who have been listening alertly, groan aloud with sympathy.

"Pascal had only one book available in the prison—a Bible provided by his family. He read it daily, and despite his atheistic beliefs, he began to pray. He found that science could not help him in a prison." (Loud laughter.) "By the end of three months, Pascal was leading a Bible study every night in that crowded room.

What does a "church" look like among lumpen people such as these, sentenced to years of misery among murderers, rapists, and drug dealers?

"Much to his surprise, Pascal was released after those three months. Someone in the government had a change in heart. But here is an amazing thing: Pascal keeps going back to prison! He visits twice each week to preach and to distribute Bibles. On Fridays he brings in huge pots of vegetable soup, because he found that the prisoners were dying of malnutrition. Many had been jailed for stealing food—they were hungry before they went in!"

The Chileans look around at each other. This story is hitting close. Ron continues.

"Pascal shows the difference Christ can make in a person's life. When you walk out of prison, you'll probably want to erase it from your mind. But Pascal couldn't do that. He believed God wanted him to go back, to share God's love that he had found in that stinking, crowded room."

After the story, the Chilean prisoners, obviously moved, break out in loud applause. Ron continues, telling story after story of people who have met Christ behind bars. Then members of the congregation stand up to speak.

One of the band members, a short, wiry man with a thick scar run-

The Church Behind Bars

ning across his left cheek, speaks first. "They used to think I was so dangerous that they kept me in chains. And I'll tell you why I first started going to prison church—I was looking for an escape hole!" Everyone laughs, even the guards. "But there I found true freedom in Christ, not just a way to escape."

Another prisoner limps to the front. He explains that he lost a leg and most of his bowels in a shooting incident in an Argentine prison. He became a Christian in 1985, he says. Shortly after that he located the man who had killed his brother. "Before, I would have killed that man," he says. "But with Christ in my heart, I was able to forgive him. Now I know I am called to preach to the others here in prison. It's a more important job than being president of General Motors. And with thirty-four years to go on my sentence, I'll have plenty of time!"

The service goes on, gathering emotional steam. Prisoners spontaneously kneel by the rough wooden benches to pray for their fellow inmates. The singing, animated with hand-clapping and foot-stomping, gets louder and more boisterous. Other prisoners abandon their basketball games and crowd around the open doorway to see what they are missing. When the foreign visitors leave, amid many hugs and handshakes, all the prisoners stay. They are just getting warmed up.

I can still hear strains of the prisoners' singing as I settle with other visitors around a long rectangular table in the prison warden's office. The warden has asked Ron Nikkel and his guests to meet with the prison's psychologist, sociologist, and social workers. Clearly, we are being shown one of Chile's showcase prisons, with modern facilities and services.

The staff professionals view the effect of Christian faith on the inmates with a spirit of benign tolerance: Sprinkle saltpeter on the inmates' toast to help control their sex drives, and why not add a small dose of religion to help control their tempers. The chaplain and other Prison Fellowship staff members, however, believe their work among inmates can contribute far more. Using statistics and case studies, they try to demonstrate that no rehabilitation scheme will work unless it takes into account the inmates' spiritual needs.

The discussion ranges along such lines for thirty minutes, at which time the prison warden crosses a tolerance threshold. In every way, the warden fulfills the perfect Hollywood stereotype of a South American military officer. His huge barrel chest serves as a perfect display board for rows and rows of multicolored military ribbons, and his shoulder epaulet sports three stars. Only a bushy moustache breaks up the stony monotony of his sallow face.

When the warden speaks, everyone else falls silent. "It doesn't matter to me which faith these prisoners take to," he announces with finality. "But it's clear they need to change, and they'll never do it without some outside assistance. Religion may give them the will to change that they could never develop on their own."

As he speaks, we can still hear the prisoners singing in the courtyard chapel. "Chaplain," he continues, "one-third of the men in this facility attend your services. You visit several times a week, but I'm here every day. And I tell you, those men are different. They don't just put on a performance when you come around—they are different than the other prisoners. They have a joy. They share with other prisoners. They care about more than themselves. And so I think we ought to do all we can to help this fine work."

The director's statement promptly ends all discussion. All the prison professionals nod their agreement. As we leave the prison, the worship service is finally breaking up. The prisoners are marching around the exercise yard in twin columns, singing hymns to the beat of drums and tambourines. I look at my watch—two hours have passed since the service began.

The taxi to downtown Santiago takes a long, circuitous route, and as we ride, Ron reflects on his day at the prison. "It never fails to get to me, no matter how many prisons I visit," he says. "To see human beings in such miserable conditions, and yet praising God. In their faces you can see a joy and love like I've encountered nowhere else. I wish some of the dispirited Christians back in North America and Europe could travel with me and see the difference Christ can make in a person's life. God chooses the weak and foolish things of the world to confound the wise and the mighty."

"I bring you greetings from your brothers and sisters in Christ in prisons around the world," Ron begins again, in another Chilean prison a day later. This one, shoehorned between buildings in urban Santiago, with an asphalt exercise yard, and cell blocks stacked vertically in high-rises, conveys a far more oppressive feeling.

The prison chapel, located in a basement, is especially gloomy. To save on energy costs, prison officials have unscrewed every other fluorescent bulb in the ceiling (even the bulbs are covered by bars). I'm beginning to wonder if prisons are designed by architects competing to produce the world's ugliest buildings. All walls are square, functional, and free of ornamentation. Surfaces consist of rough concrete or smooth iron bars, with no mediating textures like tile, carpet, or wallpaper. Prisons strip human inventions, just like human beings, to the barest essentials.

"I bring you greetings from Jose, a Filipino man I met in a Saudi Arabian jail. He was arrested for murder, and has spent the last five years in prison. The police tortured a confession out of him. He later recanted it in court, but he was convicted anyway and will probably face execution.

"Yet Jose found Christ in that Muslim jail, through a Christian cellmate. I visited his prison, a brick building with very little ventilation. It must have been 110° in there. Jose had to shout his testimony to me—visitors must sit in an area four feet away from the prisoners, who are locked in cages covered with double steel mesh. 'My time in here is hell,' Jose yelled. 'But I wouldn't trade it for anything. In this place I met Jesus!' "

As the chapel service continues, the military director of the prison motions for us to follow him. We get a hurried tour of the dreary facility through an endless maze of tunnels and iron gates. Two things stand out: the odor of a forty-year buildup of disinfectant, and the large framed faces of Chile's rulers glowering at us from many walls.

Nothing has prepared me for the director of the oldest prison in Chile. If yesterday's director was straight out of central casting, this one must be on loan from *Saturday Night Live*. He is short and thin, with an unruly shock of dark brown hair. He wears a rumpled green uniform devoid of badges, ribbons, and stars. He dashes around his office in a whirlwind, arranging chairs, showing off his display case collection of swords and knives, making little jokes. His eyebrows dance up and down as he talks, adding punctuation marks to his sentences. In facial expression and mannerisms, he reminds me of Pancho, sidekick of the Cisco Kid.

The director apologizes for a shortage of coffee cups. "I only have three," he says, winking. "Drink fast, and then I'll rinse out the cups and serve the other guests." As Ron Nikkel begins to explain Prison Fellowship to him, this funny man suddenly raises his hand to interrupt. "Ah, but we must have music!" he says. "Do you like disco music, my friends?" He rushes to an oversized white plastic cassette player with the brand name Disco Robo. A Latin rumba beat fills the room, and the director returns to his desk with a broad smile, motioning for Ron to continue.

It is a scene straight out of Kafka. Most human rights organizations rank Chilean prisons near the bottom of the scale; routinely prisoners go on hunger strike for more humane conditions. And yet we sit in the director's office at one of those prisons juggling coffee cups and tapping our toes to rumba music.

The ironies carry over into the evening. We eat dinner in one of Santiago's finest restaurants, as the guests of a wealthy man concerned about prison ministry in Chile. Around the table sit Prison Fellowship staff members, the local board, and several representatives from the government. The restaurant presents a floor show based on Easter Island themes, and soon the stage is alive with beautiful women dressed in

The Church Behind Bars

brightly colored skirts and coconut-husk tops. Shouting through translators over the din, we try to discuss prison policy.

"Sometimes I feel like a commuter," Ron Nikkel says to me the next day. "Only I commute in and out of other people's pain. Yesterday we spent the morning inside a prison full of agony. Then we dined with the men who control those prisons. That paradox tears me apart. I return home after every trip drained and perplexed. How can we work with both the oppressors and the oppressed? That's my real dilemma."

Ironically, Ron sees the utter failure of penal systems around the world as Prison Fellowship's greatest boon. "If I were to write a book about the strategy of Prison Fellowship, I would title it *Holy Subversion,*" he says. "Can we subvert the world's powers by working with their rejects, the prisoners?

"Marxists fail at their prisons, as do Muslims, Hindus, and secular humanists. Nothing works. Societies shut prisoners out of sight because they're an embarrassment, an admission of failure. But they let prison ministries in, figuring we can't worsen an already hopeless situation. And there, behind those bars in the least likely of all places, the church of God takes shape.

"It's a New Testament church in its purest form. In Chile, for example, there are five thousand different denominations and church groups! But in Chilean prisons, the Christians are one. Prison abolishes all the normal distinctions of denomination and race and class."

Furthermore, Ron said, in societies so closed that they apply the death penalty for a conversion to Christianity, prisons are opening doors to Prison Fellowship. "Nothing else has worked in those prisons, so in desperation they turn to the Christians."

We don't read about such works of God in U.S. news magazines. They report mostly on controversies within the church: scandals among evangelicals, killings of abortion doctors, protests against the pope. But something else is taking place at the grass-roots level—below the grass-roots level, even, in societies' "garbage heaps." In Northern Ireland, former IRA terrorists now take Communion alongside Protestants they once had sworn to kill. In Papua, New Guinea, prison ministry is led by a judge who used to sentence people to the jails he now visits in the name of Christ.

Bishop Desmond Tutu has said the Western world would experience a "spiritual bankruptcy" if it were deprived of the "moral capital" of its prisoners. He should know: some of his friends, distinguished spokesmen for black South Africa, spent much of their lives behind bars. Tutu links them to a lineage that includes John Bunyan, Mahatma Gandhi, Martin Luther King, Aleksandr Solzhenitsyn, and Fyodor Dostoevsky.

Thus one by-product of prison ministries is the remarkable opportunity to minister to the future leaders of the world. The most spectacular recent result of this "by-product" ministry occurred in the Philippines in the late 1970s, when the leading opposition spokesman, Benigno Aquino, was languishing in prison. Full of anger and bitterness against the Marcos regime, he used his time to study Marxism.

197

"The guards used to let the dogs eat half my dinner and then give me what was left," Aquino recalled. "I hated everyone." Then his mother sent a copy of Prison Fellowship founder Charles Colson's book *Born Again*, and Aquino found himself strangely moved by the story so full of hope. He became a Christian, and because of that hope was able to survive in prison. It was there that he developed his philosophy of nonviolent revolution.

Unexpectedly, Aquino gained his freedom in 1980, when President Marcos permitted him to travel to the U.S. for heart surgery. While there he met Colson, by coincidence, on an airplane. Colson recalls the incident: "I noticed this Oriental man staring at me, and then he grabbed my arm. 'You're Chuck Colson! Your book changed my life.' I'll never forget our conversation. Benigno told me, 'One day I will go back to the Philippines—either to serve the government or to return to prison. Either way, we'll start Prison Fellowship there. I promised that to the Lord when I walked out of prison.' "

Before leaving, Aquino studied the life of Dietrich Bonhoeffer, who returned to Germany during World War II in full awareness of the dangers. Aquino, of course, never made it past the tarmac in the Philippines. He was shot by the military as he emerged from the door of the plane. But his promise has been fulfilled. Two and a half years later, the nonviolent revolution he had set in motion swept Marcos from power. And Prison Fellowship in the Philippines is now thriving.

"I bring you greetings from your brothers and sisters in Christ in prisons around the world," Ron Nikkel says once more, to another group of prisoners. We are in Peru now, and the international travel, combined with long evening meetings with prison volunteers and embassy staff and penal authorities, has taken its toll. Ron's face wears the fatigue of the past week.

Our meeting room adjoins a row of cells, so that in addition to the sixty prisoners in our room, a few others are diffidently watching the proceedings from their beds. In prison, you learn to live with certain things: congestion, constant background noise, ever-glowing light bulbs, an utter lack of privacy. Peru's prisons are advanced enough to have a commode in each cell—it sits in the center of the cell, visible from all sides.

The prisoners in our meeting room are mostly wearing gym shorts, flip-flops, and a comical assortment of T-shirts that bear messages such as "Mailmen do it with zip," "Somebody in Utah loves me," and "Laguna Beach Country Club." Not even the barbed wire of a Third World prison can keep out American sloganeering.

Today, Ron keeps the stories short. He feels like preaching a sermon. "Did you know that Jesus Christ was a prisoner?" he asks the scruffy-looking group. From their facial expressions, it appears that, no, they did not know that. "Well, he was. Jesus came to earth so that God could experience all that we experience here, and that included going to prison.

"Do you know what it's like when someone squeals on you—turns you in to the authorities?" Vigorous affirmative nods. "Jesus felt that too. One of his best friends turned him in on a trumped-up charge. Justice was no better in his day than in ours. The government broke all the rules during his trial, and sentenced him to death.

"And when he died on the cross, a prisoner died on each side of him. One prisoner taunted him: 'If you're really the Christ, get us out of here!' I've talked to many prisoners with exactly that same attitude toward God. Some of you may be angry at God. You won't listen to him unless he gets you out. But the prisoner on the other cross had a different spirit. He said simply, 'Jesus, I'm guilty but you're innocent. Please remember me.'

"And, listen—only one person in the Bible receives a direct promise of heaven. It's a thief who lived a life of crime, who did not get baptized, and who probably never went to church. He died within hours after accepting Christ. Yet that thief lives in heaven today. Jesus guaranteed it."

Ron is warming to his audience, using hand motions, speaking with more force. The tiredness has drained away. He's preaching like a southern black preacher now, stating a Bible story in simple terms, then embellishing it. "Sometimes, when I ask a person to go with me into a prison as a volunteer, they'll say, 'No, Ron, I'm scared. I don't like hanging around thieves and murderers.' If they really feel that way, then they had better not go to heaven, because I know of at least one thief who will be there, and a few murderers too!"

The prisoners are eating it up. Ron goes through the Bible telling prison stories. A verse that talks about newness of life for Christians, 2 Corinthians 5:17, is written out on an oily, makeshift blackboard behind Ron, and he points to it. He tells of the apostle Paul and his long nights in jail. "Paul's favorite description of himself is 'a prisoner of Jesus Christ.' But how could Paul write those words about becoming a new creature when he spent so much time in rotten Roman dungeons?" Ron reads from some of Paul's prison letters—bright words, happy words. "They could keep Paul's body under lock and key," he says, "but his soul was free."

The Church Behind Bars

After half an hour of preaching to an increasingly receptive audience, Ron turns the meeting back over to the prisoners. Many of them come to the front and tell of the difference Christ has made in their lives. Judging by the prisoners' reactions, the biggest surprise is Juan. Leaning on the shoulder of a woman volunteer named Marie, Juan limps forward to tell his story. The other inmates know him well, for Juan has a reputation as a troublemaker. He limps because of a run-in with prison guards. He assaulted one of the guards, and other guards gave him a beating that broke his hand, bruised his face, and left him partially lame.

Juan speaks in a husky voice. The very act of speaking causes him great pain, and he explains why. While in solitary confinement after the beating, he somehow obtained a can of DDT insecticide and swallowed it. Guards found him in his cell, near death. After that dark night, Marie, a volunteer, began visiting Juan on a special mission: she wanted to give him a reason to live.

Marie suddenly interrupts Juan's story to explain that she herself is living on borrowed time—doctors have discovered an inoperable tumor in her stomach. She points to the kerchief wrapped around her head; radiation caused most of her hair to fall out.

She told Juan in the hospital room, "How dare you take your life when I would do anything to stay alive! You have no right—your life belongs to God." Through her witness, Juan became a Christian.

As Juan and Marie finish their story, Juan asks the sixty men around him for help in the days ahead. Other inmates will surely scoff at his conversion. The group kneels together to pray for the healing of Juan's body and the strengthening of his faith through difficult times ahead. And as they pray, a warden leads Ron and the rest of our visiting group to another circle of sixty men awaiting us in a different cell block.

Late that afternoon, as we sit in a taxi in Lima's rush-hour traffic, I ask Ron about his sermon. I have known Ron for twenty years, and I would never have expected from him such a sermon. Ron always had a cynical edge to him. Like many of his generation, he bore scars of fundamentalism that made him tentative, skeptical. I ask him what has changed.

"I came to this job with professional training in criminology, and of course I still try to incorporate everything I learned. But I have gradually become convinced that the lasting answer to prison problems is not rehabilitation, but transformation. Initially, I hesitated to use phrases like 'Christ is the answer,' but frankly, I've seen that phrase proved true. I learned certain words in childhood, but the prisoners themselves finally gave meaning to those words. They proved the reality of a theology that had been little more than a mental exercise for me. They showed me faith at its most basic.

"Jesus calls blessed those who are poor, who weep, who feel hunger, who are hated and excluded and insulted by men. That's a perfect description of many prisoners I know. But can they really be blessed, happy? To my surprise, the answer is yes. Something about the condition of severe human need makes them receptive to the grace of God. They turn to God, and they are filled. It was no accident that John Bunyan wrote *Grace Abounding unto the Chief of Sinners* while in prison.

"The very best rehabilitation programs can only offer a future hope, that life may change when the prisoners get out. Christ offers a future hope—even for those who face the death sentence—and also a present hope. He can give meaning to a life even if it must be spent in an oppressive prison. I've seen it happen too many times to doubt it."

The computer industry has something called the "table-top test." Engineers design wonderful new products: circuit boards, CD-ROM drives, optical scanners. But the real question is, Will that new product survive actual use by consumers? What will happen if it accidentally gets pushed off a table? Will it survive? For Ron, prisons have become the table-top test of the Christian faith. There, simple, tough faith is put to the test every day—by people like Juan, the Peruvian man who turned to Christ after his suicide attempt failed. The eternal truth of the gospel will be tested in his life over the next few weeks.

The Church Behind Bars

Some people try to prove the truth of the gospel in the halls of academia, battling over apologetics and theology. Others compare the size and force of Christianity against other great religions of the world. Ron Nikkel says he just keeps going to prisons. There he finds the final testing area for forgiveness and love and grace. There he finds whether Christ really is alive.

I ask Ron to think back to the worst setting he'd ever seen. I took this writing assignment to see how faith survives among people who are pressed to the limits. In the dismal prisons we had visited in Chile and Peru, who could dispute the joy we had found among inmates there? But did the pattern hold true around the world? Had he ever found a place of absolute despair, with no crack of hope? What was the ultimate "table-top test" of the gospel?

Ron thought for a moment and then told me about the time he and Chuck Colson visited a maximum security prison in Zambia. Their "guide," a former prisoner named Nego, had described a secret inner prison built inside to hold the very worst offenders. To Nego's amazement, one of the guards agreed to let him show the facility to Chuck and Ron.

"We approached a steel, cagelike building covered with wire mesh. Cells line the outside of the cage, surrounding a 'courtyard' fifteen by forty feet. Twenty-three hours of each day the prisoners are kept in cells so small that they cannot all lie down at once. For one hour they are allowed to walk around in the small courtyard. Nego had spent twelve years in those cells.

"When we approached the inner prison, we could see sets of eyes peering at us from a two-inch space under the steel gate. And when the gate swung open, it revealed squalor unlike I have seen anywhere. There were no sanitation facilities—in fact, the prisoners were forced to defecate in their food pans. The blazing African sun had heated up the steel enclosure unbearably. I could hardly breathe in the foul, stifling atmosphere of that place. How could human beings possibly live in such a place? I wondered.

"And yet, here is what happened when Nego told them who we were. Eighty of the one hundred and twenty prisoners went to the back wall and assembled in rows. At a given signal, they began singing—hymns, Christian hymns, in beautiful four-part harmony. Nego whispered to me that thirty-five of those men had been sentenced to death and would soon face execution.

"I was overwhelmed by the contrast between their peaceful, serene faces and the horror of their surroundings. Just behind them, in the darkness, I could make out an elaborate charcoal sketch drawn on the wall. It showed Jesus, stretched out on a cross. The prisoners must have spent hours working on it. And it struck me with great force, the force of revelation, that Christ was there with them, sharing their suffering, and giving them joy enough to sing in such a place.

"I was supposed to speak to them, to offer some inspiring words of faith. But I could only mumble a few words of greeting. *They* were the teachers, not I."

203

The Church Behind Bars

CHAPTER 37

Two-Handed Faith

I have gained fresh insight into the meaning of faith from an unlikely combination of sources: the writings of political dissidents and an eighteenth-century French mystic.

For many years dissidents in Eastern Europe lived under oppressive regimes that tended to promote a sense of paranoia. As the saying goes, "Just because you're paranoid doesn't mean they're not after you," and these dissidents responded appropriately. They met in secret, used code words, avoided public telephones, and published pseudonymous essays in underground papers.

In the midseventies, however, Polish and Czech intellectuals began to realize that the constant double-life had cost them dearly. Quite simply, they had lost the most basic sense of freedom and human dignity. By working in secret, always with a nervous glance over the shoulder, they had succumbed to fear, the goal of their Communist opponents all along. They made a conscious decision to change tactics.

"We will act as if we are free, at all costs," the Poles, and then the Czechs, decided. The Workers' Defense Committee in Poland began holding public meetings, often in church buildings, despite the presence of known informers. They signed articles, sometimes adding an address and phone number, and distributed newspapers openly on the street corners.

In effect, the dissidents agreed to start acting in the way they thought society should become. If you want freedom of speech, speak freely. If you want an open society, act openly. If you love the truth, tell the truth. Václav Havel, the Czech playwright, had led the way by determining to write no longer with an eye on what the authorities might approve, but to write the truth, no matter what.

The authorities did not know how to respond. Sometimes they cracked down—nearly all the dissidents spent time in prison—and sometimes they watched with a frustration bordering on helplessness. Meanwhile the dissidents' brazen tactics made it far easier for them to connect with one another and the West, and a kind of "freedom archipelago" took shape, a bright counterpart to the darkling "Gulag archipelago." In a sense, they created a free society by acting "as if" their society was free.

Most important, the new approach emboldened the dissidents themselves; they discovered that inner freedom gives sustenance even when external freedom is snatched away. Prison, after all, provides an ideal setting in which to learn to cherish freedom. Against all odds, they clung to belief in fundamental principles of truth and justice even as their governments tried to compel them to believe the opposite.

The daring philosophy spread to other places, giving courage to dissidents in China, Latin America, and South Africa. As Richard Steele wrote about his experience in a South African prison:

> The *power* of fearlessness is astonishing. I think of those who were giving me orders. They were under a real tyranny and far more the victim of it than I was. When they were yelling their orders at me, I had a vivid image of these tiny creatures assaulting my feet, wanting to demolish me with orders, while I was way above, not on their level at all. They could threaten me with anything at all and not get me, because I wasn't afraid. This was immensely liberating to me. I could be the person I was without fearing them. They had no power over me.

Remarkably, we have lived to see these dissidents triumph. An alternative kingdom of people united by ideas, a kingdom of rags, of prisoners, of poets and philosophers who convey their words in the scrawl of hand-copied *samizdat*, has toppled what seemed an impregnable fortress in country after country. Even South Africa held free elections without a violent revolution.

I vividly remember watching television news reports as the climactic nonviolent revolution took place in the streets of Moscow. Russians who had grown up in the world center of totalitarianism suddenly declared, "We will act as if we are free"—in front of the KGB building, staring down the mouths of tank cannons. I was traveling in Scandinavia that summer, and as I watched the images, lacking an English translation, I could only guess at the details of what was transpiring just across the border. The contrast between the faces of the coup leaders inside and the masses outside told me all I needed to know, though. With startling clarity, they showed who was really afraid, and who was really free.

Watching newsreels from Red Square on Finnish television, I came up with a new definition of faith: paranoia in reverse.

On this same trip I read *The Sacrament of the Present Moment*, a remarkable book by the French mystic Jean-Pierre de Caussade, translated by Kitty Muggeridge. Writing to a group of beleaguered nuns in the chaotic decades before the French Revolution, de Caussade set out for them a challenging program of spiritual direction.

"Faith gives the whole earth a celestial aspect," he said. "Each moment is a revelation of God." Regardless of how things appear at a given moment in time, all of history will ultimately serve to accomplish God's purpose on earth. He advised the nuns to "love and accept the present moment as the best, with perfect trust in God's universal goodness. . . . Everything without exception is an instrument and means of sanctification."

Objections immediately sprang to my mind, as probably happened

Two-Handed Faith

with the nuns who first read those words. *God's universal goodness* in a nation careering toward blood and madness? *A celestial aspect* in a world growing increasingly pagan? Suffering, violence, persecution—are these, too, instruments and means of sanctification?

Watching newsreels from Red Square on Finnish television, reading the hard words from de Caussade, I came up with a new definition of faith: paranoia in reverse.

A truly paranoid person organizes his or her life around a common perspective of fear. Whatever happens feeds that fear. Try to comfort a paranoiac, "I'm here to help you, not hurt you," and you will merely increase the fear. *(Of course he'd say that—he's part of the conspiracy.)*

Faith works in the reverse. A faithful person organizes his or her life around a common perspective of trust, not fear. Bedrock faith convinces me that despite the apparent chaos of the present moment, God does reign; that regardless of how cast off I may feel, I matter, truly matter, to a God of love; that no pain lasts forever and no evil triumphs in the end. Faith sees even the darkest deed of all history, the death of God's Son, as a necessary prelude to the brightest. Faith allows me to live under the reign of God even on a planet ruled by a sinister force known as "the god of this world."

Centuries ago Gregory of Nicaea called a fellow church leader's faith *ambidextrous* because he welcomed pleasures with the right hand and afflictions with the left, convinced that both would serve God's design for him. "God's purpose for us is always what will contribute most to our good," said de Caussade. Tough words. I believe them today, but will I tomorrow?

We have seen in our own time what can happen when a group of people band together to live out a truth—*we are free*—that all around them is being denounced as a lie. Walls and kingdoms crumble. What would happen if we in God's kingdom *acted as if* the words of the apostle John are literally true: "The one who is in you is greater than the one who is in the world"? What would happen if we started living *as if* the most-repeated prayer in Christendom has actually been answered, that God's will be done on earth as it is in heaven?

CHAPTER 38

Don't Forget to Laugh

The human species is distinctive in at least three ways, said poet W. H. Auden. We are the only animals who work, laugh, and pray. I have found that Auden's list provides a neat framework for self-reflection. What about Christians who live in relative freedom, security, and comfort? I wonder. If indeed faith can transform the lives of those pressed to the edge of human endurance, what about the rest of us? How do we measure up?

At *work*, Christians unabashedly excel. In Latin America, Eastern Europe, and even Communist China, opponents must grudgingly acknowledge that for all their faults Christians are industrious. Our forefathers invented the Protestant ethic, after all.

We value the work ethic so highly, in fact, that we let it gobble everything in sight. Our churches run like corporations; our quiet times fit into a Day-Timer™ schedule (ideally on computer software); our pastors maintain the hectic pace of Japanese executives. Work has become for Christians the only sanctioned addiction.

The art of *prayer* we should have mastered by now, but I have my doubts. It is tempting to turn prayer into another form of work, which may explain why prayers in most churches consist mainly of intercession. We bring God our requests in the form of wish lists, and all too rarely do we get around to listening.

I've noticed that biblical prayers (as seen, for example, in some of

209

the Psalms) tend to be wandering, repetitive, and unstructured—closer in form to the conversation you might hear in a barber shop than a shopping list. I am learning about such prayer from the Catholics, who have a better grasp on prayer as an act of worship. Oddly, for those who work at it all day—Henri Nouwen, Thomas Merton, Macrina Wiederkehr, Gerard Manley Hopkins, Teresa of Avila—prayer seems less like a chore and more like a never-ending conversation. Like ordinary life with the simple addition of an Audience.

I recall an interview Dan Rather did with Mother Teresa of Calcutta. "What do you say to God when you pray?" he asked. Mother Teresa looked at him with her dark, soulful eyes and said quietly, "I listen." Slightly flustered, Rather tried again. "Well, then, what does God say?" Mother Teresa smiled. "He listens."

In *laughter*, the third leg of Auden's triad, Christians trail behind the rest of the world. How else to explain the low circulation of a humor magazine like *The Wittenberg Door* and the angry letters Christian magazines receive from subscribers who fail to comprehend satire?

To correct the imbalance, W. H. Auden proposed resurrecting the medieval practice of Carnival, the raucous holiday preceding Lent. He writes:

> Carnival celebrates the unity of our human race as m:tal creatures, who come into this world and depart from it without our consent, who must eat, drink, defecate, belch, and break wind in order to live, and procreate if our species is to survive. Our feelings about this are ambiguous.... We oscillate between wishing we were unreflective animals and wishing we were disembodied spirits, for in either case we should not be problematic to ourselves. The Carnival solution of this ambiguity is to laugh, for laughter is simultaneously a protest and an acceptance.

In the Middle Ages, Carnival offered an outlet for expressing such ambiguity. Young men dressed up as girls, young girls as boys. Individuals hid behind masks and costumes that tended to caricature the oddity of the human animal through exaggeration and parody: false noses, elaborate hairdos, skulls, fat bellies, fanged teeth, horns.

I got caught in Mardi Gras once, smack in the middle of Bourbon Street, New Orleans, and I must say it bore little resemblance to the medieval Carnival. Young women walked through the streets yelling, "Breasts for beads!" In exchange for a gaudy plastic necklace they'd pull up their T-shirts and bare themselves. In their drunkenness, lust, and even violence, the revelers at Mardi Gras were not parodying but rather groveling in their animalness.

> Laughter
> has much in common
> with prayer.

The descent from the church's Carnival to the debauchery of Mardi Gras is a theological descent. As G. K. Chesterton put it, "If it is not true that a divine being fell, then one can only say that one of the animals went completely off its head." That, precisely, is where Christians part company with modern materialists. Carnival parodies a divine being who fell; Mardi Gras celebrates an animal gone completely off its head.

C. S. Lewis once said that in the absence of any other evidence, the essentials of natural theology could be argued from the human phenomena of dirty jokes and attitudes toward death. Dirty jokes dwell almost exclusively on the subjects of excretion and reproduction, two of the most "natural" processes on earth; yet in our smirks and double entendres we treat them as utterly unnatural, even comical. Try to envision a horse or cow bashful about the need to excrete in public. Or imagine a dog or cat with sexual hangups, reluctant to mate. Functions that we share with all other animals somehow, to humans alone, seem strange. Similarly, the only good reason to find humor in such phenomena as oversized noses and the belching reflex is that we still retain the faintest echo of Eden. In some deep and ambiguous manner of instinct, it seems odd to us that we upright vertebrates, tipped with a divine flame, act so much like other vertebrates.

As for death, only we humans treat it with shock and revulsion, as though we can't get used to the reality, universal though it may be. Every culture devises elaborate ceremonies to mark the final passage of a human being. Even those of us in the Christian West, with our traditional belief in an afterlife, dress up our corpses in new suits, embalm them (for what, posterity?), and bury them in airtight caskets and concrete vaults. In these rituals we act out a stubborn reluctance to yield to this most powerful of human experiences. As Lewis suggests, these anomalies betray a permanent state of tension within human beings. An individual person is a spirit made in the image of God but merged temporarily with a body of flesh, and dirty jokes and an obsession with death express a rumbling sense of discord about this in-between state. We lack unity because long ago a gap fissured open between our mortal and immortal parts; theologians trace the fault line back to the Fall.

Christians have a great advantage over other people, C. S. Lewis continued: not by being less fallen than they or less doomed to live in a fallen world, but by knowing that they are fallen creatures in a fallen world. For this reason, I think, we dare not forget how to laugh at ourselves. I have read some of the classical materialists—Charles Darwin, Karl Marx, and Bertrand Russell—and I have yet to find the slightest curve of a smile lurking among their words. The "politically correct" movement of our time shows a similar solemnity. One can only parody what one respects, just as one can only blaspheme if one believes.

It occurs to me, in fact, that laughter has much in common with prayer. In both acts, we stand on equal ground, freely acknowledging ourselves as fallen creatures. We take ourselves less seriously. We think of our creatureliness. Work divides and ranks; laughter and prayer unite.

W. H. Auden ends his reflection with this warning:

A satisfactory human life, individually or collectively, is possible only if proper respect is paid to all three worlds. Without Prayer and Work, the Carnival laughter turns ugly, the comic obscenities grubby and pornographic, the mock aggression into real hatred and cruelty. Without Laughter and Work, Prayer turns Gnostic, cranky, Pharisaic, while those who try to live by Work alone, without Laughter or Prayer, turn into insane lovers of power, tyrants who would enslave Nature to their immediate desire—an attempt which can only end in utter catastrophe, shipwreck on the Isle of the Sirens.

CHAPTER 39

Saints and Semi-Saints

The biblical characters Ezra and Nehemiah, exact contemporaries, faced the same leadership challenge. Each sought to revive dispirited refugees in Jerusalem by persuading them to rebuild city walls and clean up their morals. But what different tactics the two men used!

When Ezra arrived in Jerusalem and saw firsthand the moral degeneration of his people, he went into a state of shock. He tore his clothes, yanked hair from his head and beard, and sat down appalled. Hours later, Ezra was still weeping and throwing himself on the ground. So demonstrative was his grief and so infectious his repentance that the city leaders all agreed to change their ways.

Nehemiah, who arrived on the scene a few years later, used a more confrontational approach. As merchants lined up outside the city to sell goods on the Sabbath, he threatened them with physical violence. And when fellow Jews married foreigners against God's command, he called down curses on them, beat them, and pulled out their hair.

That last scene highlights the difference between the two biblical heroes: one pulls out his own hair in grief; another pulls out other people's hair in anger.

Ezra was a priest, a mystic. He had refused an armed escort for the eight-hundred-mile journey from Babylon to Jerusalem despite the fact that his group of émigrés carried twenty-eight tons of silver. Concerned that the presence of armed guards might demonstrate a lack of faith, he chose to rely instead on fasting and prayer for protection.

Nehemiah, a bureaucrat of exquisite pragmatism, had no such scruples. He entered Jerusalem at the head of a Persian cavalry detachment, and at the first sign of opposition he organized the Jews, too, into armed battalions. Soon every workman on the wall was carrying a weapon in his free hand.

Ezra and Nehemiah got me thinking about the different approaches people take in living out their Christian faith. If Ezra was a saint, Nehemiah was a semi-saint.

A *saint* (as I am using the term) is a radical, a moral extremist who shuns all compromise and may well look foolish in the eyes of the world. Mother Teresa stands in the center of one of the most crowded cities on earth and lectures against birth control. "Every baby is a gift from God," she says. Thirty years ago, Martin Luther King, Jr., would seek out the meanest sheriffs in Alabama and Mississippi and plant his unarmed body directly in the path of their dogs and fire hoses. His goal, King used to say, was not to defeat the white man, but "to awaken a sense of shame within the oppressor," and the best way to shame a nation was to fight violence with aggressive nonviolence.

The church has seen some effective *semi-saints* as well. William Wilberforce became the butt of many jokes in eighteenth-century England because of his one-note-band speeches in Parliament against slavery. But in the end, his "bureaucratic faithfulness" helped carry the day, and England chose the way of moral courage, even agreeing to compensate slave owners in the colonies. In our own country Abraham Lincoln believed, truly believed, that he would serve God best by pursuing a terrible war to its bitter end.

My writing career has afforded me the chance to observe a few contemporary "saints." Some have left comfortable homes in North America to witness for peace in Central America or to serve in squalid refugee camps in Africa; others spend their lives sheltering and feeding America's urban homeless. After talking to these people, I go away inspired, ennobled, and filled with a higher vision of what a Christian can be.

I have also met some semi-saints. Every working day Christian lobbyists put on three-piece suits and traipse over to Capitol Hill to represent the interests of starving children and aborted babies and maltreated prisoners and victims of human rights abuses. These semi-saints may play a less glamorous role, but can anyone doubt that an organization like Bread for the World accomplishes as much on behalf of the poor and hungry as does, say, Mother Teresa?

> Although we need saints, desperately, they will probably always be a rare breed.

In India today some "holy men" are leading a campaign against deforestation. These visionaries encourage villagers to tie themselves to trees in order to block the loggers and their chain saws. Television crews flock to cover the dramatic scene of protest (a cause that I, for one, support). But the saintly protest in India might not even be necessary if every semi-saint in America would diligently recycle envelopes and daily newspapers.

Although we need saints, desperately, they will probably always be a rare breed. The vast majority of Christians in this country work at "secular" jobs from nine to five each day, worship on Sundays, and try to let their faith influence their lives. Such folks may never enjoy the singular vision, or perhaps the freedom from ambiguity, that characterizes a genuine saint. But I take comfort in the fact that the Bible seems to allow for both approaches.

Ezra and Nehemiah, telling the same story from two points of view, make clear that neither approach is entirely effective on its own. Nehemiah, the obsessive, management-oriented bureaucrat, completed in fifty-two days a mission that Ezra had failed to accomplish in a dozen years: he got a wall built around Jerusalem to provide security for the residents inside.

On the other hand, once the construction project was completed, Nehemiah turned to Ezra to lead the religious celebration. The latter part of Nehemiah depicts that day as one of the most remarkable scenes of Old Testament history. A vast throng of refugees assembled in a huge plaza, and Ezra read from the Law from daybreak until noon. Working in tandem, the two leaders—Nehemiah with his no-nonsense pragmatism and Ezra with his unimpeachable integrity—directed a spiritual revival such as had not been seen in a thousand years. In that revival, both saints and semi-saints played a part.

CHAPTER 40

In Search of a Both/And Church

Not long ago I attended a conference held on the restored grounds of a century-old Utopian community in Indiana. As I ran my fingers over the fine workmanship of the buildings and read the plaques describing the daily lives of the true believers, I marveled at the energy that drove this movement, one of dozens spawned by American idealism and religious fervor.

Many varieties of perfectionism have grown on American soil: offshoots from the Second Great Awakening, the Victorious Life movement, communes of the Jesus movement. It occurred to me, though, that in recent times the perfectionist urge has virtually disappeared. Nowadays we tilt in the opposite direction, toward a kind of anti-utopianism. For example, as a result of the recovery movement, many churches formed twelve-step groups around the theme of addiction to sex, food, alcohol, or drugs; these groups by definition center on members' *inability* to be perfect.

I confess my preference for this modern trend. I observe far more human fallibility than perfectibility, and I have cast my lot with a gospel based on grace. Yet in New Harmony, Indiana, I felt an unaccountable nostalgia for the Utopians: all those solemn figures in black clothes breaking rocks in the fields, devising ever-stricter rules in an attempt to rein in lust and greed, striving to fulfill the lofty commands of the New Testament. The mere names they left behind are enough to break your heart: New Harmony, Peace Dale, New Hope, New Haven.

The Catholic church has bred its share of perfectionism as well. I have studied the rule of Saint Benedict and read the stirring accounts of early Jesuit missionaries who sailed to Japan and China. Compared with such discipline and dedication, the current wave of short-term missions seems like a consumer fad. What will we moderns leave behind for future generations to ponder? I wondered. The names that came to mind were hardly inspiring: Codependency Dale, New Vulnerability, New Sharing.

Yet most Utopian communities—like the one I was standing in —survive only as museums. Perfectionism keeps running aground on the barrier reef of original sin.

A few years back a book by Douglas Frank, *Less Than Conquerors*, offered an insightful analysis of the pitfalls of perfectionism. Charles G. Trumbull, a leader in the Victorious Life movement, once said, "It is the privilege of every Christian to live every day of his life without breaking the laws of God in known sin either in thought, word or deed." Such high ideals, observes Frank, paradoxically lead to despair and defeatism. Despite all good efforts, human beings don't achieve a state of sinlessness, and in the end they often blame themselves (a blame encouraged by their leaders: "If it is not working, you must not be believing enough").

Frank points out yet another flaw in perfectionism: too often it disintegrates into pettiness (one of the sharpest criticisms Jesus made of the Pharisees). In an attempt to dilute the delights of the flesh, Charles Finney's Oberlin College banned coffee, tea, pepper, mustard, oil, and vinegar. The experiment didn't last long, as any recent visitor to Oberlin can attest.

I grew up in a climate of severe perfectionism from which I have spent much of life recovering, and I learned firsthand the pettiness of modern fundamentalism. My church debated the morality of bowling alleys ("Don't they serve liquor?") and roller-skating ("They hold hands!") but cared not a whit about human rights in South Africa or civil rights at home in Georgia.

FINDING GOD in Unexpected PLACES

Still, despite a potent inoculation against the abuses of perfectionism, I sometimes feel this nostalgia, even longing, for the quest itself. I read with amazement Thomas Merton's *Ascent to Truth*, which chronicles one man's full-time search for mystical union with God. I burn with shame as I read the Russian classic *The Way of a Pilgrim*, which tells of a peasant who took literally the command, "Pray without ceasing," and prayed the Jesus prayer ("Lord Jesus Christ, Son of God, have mercy on me, a sinner") seven thousand times a day.

> I grew up in a climate of severe perfectionism from which I have spent much of life recovering.

How can we in the church uphold the ideal of holiness, the proper striving for Life on the Highest Plane, while avoiding the consequences of disillusionment, pettiness, abuse of authority, spiritual pride, and exclusivism?

221

Or, to ask the opposite question, how can we moderns who emphasize community support (never judgment), vulnerability, and introspection keep from aiming too low? An individualistic society, America is in constant danger of freedom abuse; its churches are in danger of grace abuse.

With these questions in mind, I read through most of the New Testament Epistles, though in a different order than usual. First I read Galatians, with its magnificent charter of Christian liberty and its fiery pronouncements against petty legalism. "It is for freedom that Christ has set us free," Paul declared (5:1). But three paragraphs later he added these words: "But do not use your freedom to indulge the sinful nature; rather, serve one another in love."

Next I turned to James, the "right strawy epistle" that stuck in Martin Luther's throat. I was familiar with James's stern admonitions, but I had not noticed his formula for obtaining holiness. James balanced each prodding to "strive harder" with the simple advice to depend on God (1:5, 17, 21; 4:3, 7; 5:11). "Mercy triumphs over judgment!" he concluded.

I read Ephesians and then 1 Corinthians, Romans and then 1 Timothy, Colossians and then 1 Peter. In every book without exception I found both messages: the high ideals of holiness and also the safety net of grace, a merciful reminder that salvation does not depend on our meeting those ideals. Ephesians pulls the two strands together neatly: "For it is by grace you have been saved, through faith—and this not from yourselves, it is the gift of God—not by works, so that no one can boast. For we are God's workmanship, created in Christ Jesus to do good works, which God prepared in advance for us to do."

I took some comfort in the fact that the church in the first century was already on a seesaw, tilting now toward perfectionistic legalism and now toward raucous antinomianism. James wrote to one extreme; Paul often addressed the other. Each letter had a strong correcting emphasis, but all stressed the dual message of the gospel. The church, in other words, should be both: a people who strive toward holiness and yet relax in grace, a people who condemn themselves but not others, a people who depend on God and not themselves.

The seesaw is still lurching back and forth. Some churches tilt one way, some another. My reading of the Epistles left me yearning for a both/and church. I have seen too many either/or congregations.

CHAPTER 41

Having a Bad Hymn Day

or a number of Sunday mornings in a row, I began the day by reading from John Milton's *Paradise Lost*. The language was thrilling, the images ethereal, the themes exalted. Then I proceeded to church, a congregation that sings "praise songs" accompanied by a keyboard and guitars. Without fail, someone requested the children's favorite, "Our God Is an Awesome God," which contains the eminently forgettable line, "When He rolls up His sleeves, He ain't just puttin' on the Ritz."

For me, the jarring descent from *Paradise Lost* to "Awesome God" has come to symbolize a major dilemma of aesthetics. How does one appreciate quality without becoming a snob? About some things, I have no snobbery: I wear hand-me-down clothes, stay in budget motels, and drive a boxy, practical car. But I can instantly sniff the difference between coffee brewed by Mr. Coffee™ and that brewed by Braun™. And when it comes to music, I'll always vote for Bach and Mozart over songs built around three major chords and a dull phrase repeated over and over.

How do we encourage Bach while not quenching the spirit of "Kum Ba Yah"? How to appreciate Milton without scorning gospel tracts? Or, to broaden the issue, how do we recognize quality of any type—physical beauty, intelligence, athletic ability—without devaluing those who lack such gifts?

Our world rewards the gifted at the expense of the less gifted. Stand outside a kindergarten playground and watch how children treat playmates who seem clumsy, ugly, or dense. Adults continue the pattern. We pay professional athletes $5 million a year and teachers $30,000. We choose young girls of promising beauty, starve them, pad them, and carve them with a plastic surgeon's knife to transform them into Supermodels who will then leave less-endowed females (99.9 percent of the population) with a permanent self-image crisis.

The church has wavered back and forth on the issue of values. Those who followed the *via negativa*, or Negative Way, solved the problem by renouncing all sensual pleasures. They ate diets of bread and water, lashed themselves with whips, and rigorously practiced celibacy. (A neglected side of celibacy: If no one gets married, then no one feels left out, either.) Jerome, an outstanding proponent of this school in the fourth century, had a stunted aesthetic sense but had much time for prayer, worship, and acts of discipline. As I have already mentioned, he sublimated his sexual drive by translating the Hebrew Scriptures, which resulted in the Vulgate version used for the next millennium.

Augustine, Jerome's contemporary, took a different approach. He had a keen eye for beauty, enjoyed a good Roman feast, and worked to improve his body, mind, and soul. Augustine believed in the essential goodness of created things; the Latin phrase *dona bona*, or "good gifts," appears throughout his *City of God.* The trick, as he saw it, was to maintain a balance between the values of the City of God and the city of this world. "The world is a smiling place," he preached once in a sermon.

Naked stylites who live on poles and ermine-draped bishops who live in palaces point to different ways of resolving the aesthetic dilemma. Today, some churches play Bach on organs more magnificent than Johann himself could have imagined. Others accompany "Awesome God" with a forty-piece orchestra. Still others ban music altogether. I once attended a wedding in which the scratchy strains of Mendelssohn's "Wedding March" came from a turntable positioned well outside the sanctuary; a long extension cord allowed them to circumvent the denominational rule against musical instruments in the church.

If Christian history offers any clue, I doubt anyone will soon come up with a neat formula to resolve these matters. But I do believe that Christianity, and only Christianity, has three essential contributions to make.

> How do we encourage Bach while not quenching the spirit of "Kum Ba Yah"?

1. Good things are a gift, not a possession. Augustine got it right with his phrase *dona bona*. We are creatures who have been "loaned" talent, beauty, and intelligence by a Creator who intended us to use them well. Created things still retain glimmers of essential goodness, hints of a divine origin. G. K. Chesterton draws the analogy of Robinson Crusoe on a rock island tenderly collecting the few comforts he could snatch from the sea, sacred relics of a sinking ship.

2. In this fallen world, good things are remnants that have been spoiled. The human Fall changed everything, and now every good thing presents an implicit risk as well, and contains within it the potential for exploitation and abuse. Think of sex, of food, of our planet's grand resources. Power, beauty, and brilliance are all good things, qualities possessed by our Creator, but human history amply demonstrates what can happen to these in the hands of human beings who have tasted of the tree of the knowledge of good and evil.

3. Even spoiled things can be made good. I have observed in art museums that saints are rather ugly, portrayed with gaunt faces, aquiline noses, and scraggly hair. I do not know whether they chose a path that led them to sainthood because of social ostracism (just as many researcher scientists—and writers, for that matter—are bookish introverts), or

whether their appearance suffered as the demands of sainthood took a physical toll. Regardless, saints by definition bear out a lasting truth of the Sermon on the Mount: God judges by different standards, and the poor and lowly, who suffer disadvantage in the city of man, have a real advantage in the City of God. Consider the heroes of Jesus' stories: the shabby beggar Lazarus, a widow with two pennies to her name, a despicable tax collector. Consider the end of Jesus' own story: from a brutal execution came the salvation of the world.

I take comfort in the fact that Christianity, while honoring God's good gifts, still finds an esteemed place for those who lack them. In the City of God, a paralyzed Joni Eareckson Tada leaps and dances with Olympian grace. And as for my original quandary about music in church, I am trying to learn a lesson from C. S. Lewis, who wrote this about his (Anglican!) church:

> I disliked very much their hymns, which I considered to be fifth-rate poems set to sixth-rate music. But as I went on I saw the great merit of it. . . . I realized that the hymns (which were just sixth-rate music) were, nevertheless, being sung with devotion and benefit by an old saint in elastic-side boots in the opposite pew, and then you realize that you aren't fit to clean those boots. It gets you out of your solitary conceit.

CHAPTER 42

Dear Mr. Chicken: Please Send Money

For a period of one month, I tossed every fund-raising appeal from the day's mail into a large box. Then I emptied and read the contents of that box: sixty-two separate appeals, weighing a total of 3.5 pounds. It terrified me. Without my immediate help, the world may come crashing down sometime next week.

First I perused the political appeals, an assortment of phony surveys and fake telegrams. The political fortunes of Jesse Helms and Strom Thurmond alarmed liberal politicians, whereas conservatives seemed preoccupied with Bill Clinton and his cohorts.

Next came a series of appeals from environmental causes (including my favorite, Friends of the Musk Ox). Unless I act, miners and loggers will despoil Alaska's remaining wilderness, zebra mussels will swallow Lake Michigan, and old growth forests will fall to the chain saws. (How many young growth forests die to provide paper for the fund-raising packets designed to save old growth forests?)

The rest of the stack of mail, more than two-thirds of the total, came from religious groups. Some years ago I gave money to an organization aiding Soviet dissidents, who happened to be Jewish. Now Simon Wiesenthal is one of my most faithful correspondents, and I also receive appeals from obscure Jewish organizations. Consider this letter from Judge Wapner, formerly presider over "People's Court," now writing on behalf of the National Institute for Jewish Hospice: "Have you ever walked past a poor old soul lying on a gurney in a cold hospital corridor? . . . Her pallid cheeks are sunken, her hair white and lifeless, her bones almost without flesh."

I got appeals from Catholic orders, too. The Passionist Monastery assured me that for a minimum ten-dollar contribution I can have twelve loved ones in Purgatory remembered in a special Mass on All Souls' Day. Or I could send my money to Servants of the Paraclete to assist with rehabilitation of fallen priests and Brothers—a growth industry, apparently.

By far the majority of the stack, however, bore the return addresses of evangelical organizations. What struck me first is how closely they resembled the appeals from everybody else: the same fake "Expressgrams" with the red "URGENT!" headlines, the same P.S.'s underlined in blue ink, the same "challenge grants" that require me to act within ten days if I want my donation to double in value. These folks must all attend the same seminars.

An editor at *Time* magazine once figured out that one complete direct mail package, including postage and list rental, costs about twenty-six cents. The cost increases if the letter is personalized, "Dear Mr. Yancey." This personalization, by the way, is an inexact science. My neighbor, Popeye's Chicken, gets letters addressed, "Dear Mr. Chicken." The Assembly of God headquarters once got a letter with the greeting "Dear Ms. God."

Many people don't know that when an organization rents lists to prospect for new donors, perhaps only one in a hundred people will respond. (This practice, called "cold prospecting," is not to be confused with Arctic mining activities.) Thus it may cost the organization twenty-six dollars to extract your first twenty-five-dollar contribution. The *Time* editor perniciously sent five-dollar donations to organizations he opposed, such as the NRA, just to watch them spend many times that amount trying to squeeze more dollars out of him.

I oppose that editor's clever but wasteful suggestion, and I am trying hard not to be cynical about this whole business of fund-raising. After all, I have written fund-raising letters myself, and I sympathize with an organization's need to communicate to donors. Indeed, the reason I receive so many fund-raising letters is that I support worthwhile organizations and respond to their appeals.

But when is enough enough? After reading sixty-two appeal letters in a row, I was impressed mainly by all the gimmicks employed. A group soliciting money for Bibles for Russia had a catchy red "Approved: Government of Russia" stamp on the envelope. One Christian television station promised me a miracle if I would give a multiple of seven: $7.77, $77.77, or $777.77; the largest amount also earns me a framed

> I am trying hard not to be cynical about this whole business of fund-raising.

original page from a 1564 Bible. A friend of mine wrote this station back, suggesting that they send him the contribution and let God reward them instead of him with the large multiple of blessings they had promised.

I had accumulated a large collection of VHS tapes highlighting the work of various missions before I finally broke down and bought a VCR machine. (To my chagrin, most of them were only ten minutes long and could not be recycled or used for taping.) One of those organizations also graciously sent me a check for $1,500. Alas, I discovered the check was made out not to me, but to the organization who sent it, as a crafty way of underscoring a challenge grant. "This facsimile check is valid only if accompanied by a check of equal or greater amount from Mr. & Mrs. Philip D. Yancey."

One mission boasts about its practice of never asking for money directly. It's funny, though, how many urgent "prayer requests" I get from them, asking me to pray for, say, the desperately needed total of $16,000 by March 1. I have the utmost respect for OMF, successor to the old China Inland Mission, which actually does follow a rigorous policy of never asking for funds. It took me several weeks to track down their address, and I've never gotten an appeal from them since!

Fund-raising appeals tend to follow current events, and it appears the Middle East and Africa have now replaced Eastern Europe as the crises of choice. Whereas a few years ago I was being asked to help distribute Bibles in Red Square and save AIDS children in Romania, now I am asked to support refugees in Sudan and Rwanda and sponsor translation of a children's Bible storybook into Arabic ("Exact locations cannot be revealed because disclosure may be life-threatening").

A letter from the American Leprosy Mission evoked much sympathy, but perhaps not for the reasons its senders intended: I felt sad for an organization that must faithfully do battle against such an old-fashioned problem. Although there are twelve million persons with leprosy in the world, the disease never makes the "hot" list in anyone's catalog of emergencies. Which brings up another problem. Any foreign-aid organization will tell you that sewers and clean water supplies have far more impact on health than a crash program of doctors and medical supplies—but try to raise money for a sewer system!

In order to get some perspective on this issue, I turned to 2 Corinthians 8–9 and read the longest fund-raising appeal in the Bible. It is a masterpiece of pressure diplomacy. The apostle Paul heaps praise on the generous Macedonians in hopes of stirring the competitive instincts of his target audience, the Corinthians. He holds up the ultimate example of Jesus: "Though he was rich, yet for your sakes he became poor." He lauds the Corinthians in advance for their anticipated gift.

Yet here is a very strange thing. I search these chapters in vain for any clue as to what the Corinthians are being asked to give *for*. Paul directs attention not to the Jews threatened by famine near Jerusalem (Romans 15:25), but to the comfortable donors themselves. He spotlights not the needy recipients (starving Jewish children in the desert), but rather the donors (spiritually enriched believers in Corinth).

In Paul's passage, the only urgent pleading comes from other donors who "urgently pleaded with us for the privilege of sharing in this service to the saints." What makes giving a privilege? Paul extols giving as a spiritual discipline that demonstrates the sincerity of Christian love, follows in the footsteps of Christ, and honors the Lord himself. As a final bonus, giving offers an outstanding witness to the watching world: "Men will praise God for the obedience . . . and for your generosity."

God loves a cheerful giver, not a reluctant one, Paul declares in this passage. No wonder. Once we understand giving's value *to ourselves*, not to the recipients, we can't help sneaking a grin. Giving, like love, never diminishes us, for blessings redound upon the happy donor. In Paul's words, giving helps to "enlarge the harvest of your righteousness."

After reading Paul's letter, I went back through all sixty-two appeals for my funds. Not a single one took the high road of focusing on my need as a Christian to honor and obey God by fulfilling his command. The benefits they mentioned were much more temporal: a photo calendar, my name in an honor roll of contributors, a listing in the annual report, a free book worth $14.95.

So who's right, the fund-raising experts who have concluded that American Christians are too self-interested to respond to any such high-minded appeals, or the apostle Paul, who broke every fund-raising rule in the book? If only we had the donor records from Corinth. . . .

CHAPTER 43

Christian McCarthyism

E ach year I join twenty other Christian writers for a weekend of
intellectual and spiritual stimulation. Aware that freelance writers don't have natural colleagues, we meet together annually for
support and encouragement.

Conversation around the dining table usually ranges from "What are
you reading these days?" to gossip about the publishing industry. Recently,
however, a cloud hung over the conversation. Several of us in the group
were under vicious attack—not from secular humanists or fundamentalist Muslims, but from fellow members of the Christian community.

Karen Mains's career as a writer and broadcaster was threatened by
a boycott over what some perceived as Jungian influences in her accounts
of her dream life. In addition, critics faulted her for citing Catholic writers such as Julian of Norwich, and for hosting Catholics on radio and TV
broadcasts.

Eugene Peterson's "tampering with God's Word" in his New Testament paraphrase, *The Message,* had made him the target of a self-
proclaimed cult-watcher. Richard Foster had dared to use words like *meditation* in his writings on spiritual discipline, which put him under
suspicion as a New Ager. Madeleine L'Engle, according to these same critics, was solidly ensconced in the New Age camp. Didn't she dabble in modern physics and imaginative literature, write about time travel, and openly
confess to repeating the "Jesus prayer" as advocated by a Russian mystic?

Other writers not present, I knew, had undergone similar attack. Tony Campolo had suffered a smear campaign in which Christians printed up scurrilous pamphlets allegedly from Queer Nation in order to cast Campolo in the worst possible light. Chuck Colson told me the ugliest mail he has ever received came from Christians in response to his accepting the Templeton Prize for Progress in Religion. "Our brethren were far less charitable than the secular media during the days of Watergate," he said. What an indictment! Yet another author told me a Christian book distributor had refused to carry a book in France that quotes from C. S. Lewis, who evidently has joined the enemies list posthumously.

I freely confess that I have not read or heard every word written or spoken by these folks. Perhaps they did say something that deserves scrutiny and even admonishment. (As a writer, I know how easy it is to write something I later regret.) What bothers me, though, is the vicious tone of the attacks, which are often dripping with sarcasm and angry invective. Campolo, Colson, Foster, L'Engle, Lewis, Mains, Peterson—are these really the "enemies" of the kingdom?

234

W hat has infected the Christian community with such an attitude of paranoia and outright meanness? The tactics used by some of these critics remind me of the worst attacks of Joseph McCarthy and Carl McIntire, my heroes as I grew up in southern fundamentalism. It was only later that I learned to recognize their conspiracy theories as a house of cards based on rumor, innuendo, and guilt by association.

I sense the same dynamic at work today. For example, I heard a nationally syndicated broadcast in which I was darkly accused of attending the Chicago Declaration II Conference in 1993, where books were sold that "cheerfully talked about incorporating voodoo practices into Holy Communion." I found this account most interesting, since not only had I barely heard of the conference, I had spent that entire month in Australia and New Zealand, halfway around the globe from Chicago.

What are we doing to each other? His last night on earth, Jesus prayed the magnificent prayer recorded in John 17, in which he asked above all for unity in his body, "to let the world know that you sent me." Are we now making a mockery of his prayer? What message are we sending the watching world?

Of course we need to hold ourselves accountable to biblical and moral principles. I worry, however, about the massive energies going into the current attacks on fellow members of Christ's body. The campaign diverts energies from the church's main function of presenting the gospel. And it confirms the skeptics' worst suspicions about the church.

> What has infected the Christian community with such an attitude of paranoia and outright meanness?

I recently read several biographies of evangelist Billy Graham, and I came away amazed at his response to opposition. Graham rose to prominence in the days of the original McCarthyism and the original McIntireism. He was savaged for inviting Catholics onto his platform, for golfing with John Kennedy, for meeting with Jews and liberal Christians, for traveling to Communist countries. He met all vituperation with soft words, humility, and a gentle spirit. Eventually, Graham's irenic spirit provided an umbrella that sheltered—and helped to mature—the entire evangelical movement. What will happen to that movement when Graham's peacemaking spirit is no longer with us?

As I reflected on the New McCarthyism in Christ's body, I recalled an editorial printed in *The Wittenberg Door* nearly two decades ago, which told of a Cub Scout camping trip in the woods of California. After swapping stories of the ferocious, Scout-eating "Bigfoot" that roamed the forest, the boys finally retired into a crowded, ten-person tent at 3:00 A.M. One boy awoke with a full bladder a few hours later and fumbled his way toward the tent flap, but was too scared to open the flap and step outdoors. The next morning the other boys awoke to find their sleeping bags soaked in urine. The boy was so scared of the real enemy, the monster outside, that he ended up soiling his neighbors.

The Door drew the application to divisions in the church, and that earthy analogy applies even more so today. Has our increasingly violent and pagan society so frightened us that we have forgotten the real enemies are outside, not inside the tent?

It is time for us to realize that differences need not lead to division. It is time for us to remember that Jesus named *love*, not theological or political correctness, as the identifying mark of Christians. "By this all men will know that you are my disciples, if you love one another."

Once, Jesus' disciples learned of an "outsider" doing the work of the kingdom. "We urged him to stop," they told Jesus, "because he was not one of us." Jesus gave this reply, one worthy of much contemplation: "Do not stop him . . . for whoever is not against us is for us."

CHAPTER 44

A Blueprint for Doomsday

As Easter approaches each year, my thoughts turn to the events of the week that was at once the most solemn and joyous of Jesus' life on earth. Palm Sunday, the Last Supper, Good Friday, Easter Sunday—all these have a settled place in the church's mystic chords of memory, but one event stands out in jarring contrast. It wears the grand label "Olivet Discourse" but "Doomsday Outburst" would be more accurate (Luke 21; Mark 13; Matthew 24).

One of Jesus' disciples has just made an innocent observation about the massive stones supporting Herod's temple: "Some rocks!"—the kind of passing comment you hear from any slack-jawed pilgrim visiting the big city. Out of nowhere, Jesus unleashes one of his longest speeches, a blend of startling images and commentary about what lies ahead for the disciples and for planet earth.

Those huge stones will be thrown down—every one of them, Jesus says. More, earthquakes and famines will break out, stars will fall from the sky, and the sun and moon will darken. "Pray that this will not take place in winter, because those will be days of distress unequaled from the beginning, when God created the world, until now—and never to be equaled again."

I can imagine the disciples, fresh from the triumph of Palm Sunday and the thrill of the temple cleansing, looking at each other in astonishment. What brought this on?

Commentators tend to focus on the details of the speech: the meaning of the wondrous bleak phrase "abomination that causes desolation," the identity of false prophets and messiahs, the exact signs that will usher in the world's last night. As I read Jesus' words, however, I am mainly struck by their emotional force, not the details. The Olivet Discourse seems more right-brained than left-brained in its approach to prophecy. As such, it offers striking clues to Jesus' emotional state as he nears his own time of trauma.

Jesus' *anxiety* comes through, surely, in this speech delivered a few days before his arrest and torture. I find it oddly comforting to read further and see that Jesus responded to pain much like I do: he felt scared, and wanted it to go away. He did not pray, "Thank you, Father, for this opportunity to suffer," but rather, "Take this cup from me." Three times he so pled with the Father, and as he prayed his sweat fell to the ground like drops of blood. Hebrews adds that Jesus prayed "with loud cries and tears to the one who could save him from death" (5:7). But Jesus would not be saved from death, and that awareness must have been ticking like a time bomb inside him on the Mount of Olives.

I sense behind Jesus' words a tone of *compassion* as well. "Flee to the mountains," he cries in alarm. "How dreadful it will be in those days for pregnant women and nursing mothers!" he sighs. Novelist Mary Gordon recalls first hearing these words in church during adolescence. Immediately she was drawn to Jesus' instinctive concern for women. "I knew I wanted children. I felt those words were for me. Now I think: how many men would take into consideration the hardships of pregnancy and nursing." She goes on to say that in her opinion Jesus is "the only affectionate hero in literature."

Jesus' compassion for his disciples shines through most darkly. "You will be handed over to be persecuted and put to death," he says, spelling out the grim future of torture and humiliation awaiting them. Reading his descriptions, I cannot push from my mind a haunting scene from the novel *Silence,* by Shusako Endo. A Portuguese missionary priest, bound, is forced to watch as samurai guards torture Japanese Christians, one by one, and throw them into the sea. The samurai swear they will keep on killing Christians until the priest re- nounces his faith. "He had come to this country to lay down his life for other men, but instead of that the Japanese were laying down their lives one by one for him."

What was it like for Jesus, who saw with piercing vision the terrible conse- quences of what he had set loose in the world not only for himself but for the huddled few around him, his best friends in all the world? "Brother will betray brother to death, and a father his child. . . . All men will hate you because of me."

> Jesus told us just enough about the future to keep us on tiptoe, watching and hoping.

Finally, I detect in the Olivet Discourse a faint advance echo of *an- ticipation:* "At that time men will see the Son of Man coming in clouds with great power and glory." Jesus' words grow fierce as he describes the cosmic turmoil that will herald the end of the world.

Sometimes we who read the Bible's cryptic passages on "the last days" end up feeling more confused than comforted. But as I read Jesus' words in context, delivered just days before his death, I better understand why the Bible includes them and why Jesus must pronounce them. He, the Lamb who lays down his own life, dare not leave his cowed disciples without a preview of the future. The Lamb will return, he promises, this time in power and glory, to put a decisive end to the struggle that has not ceased since Eden—the very struggle that menaces these his beloved friends.

Revelation uses the oxymoronic phrase "wrath of the Lamb" to describe that future visitation. Creation will convulse in one last paroxysm of pain as evil is cast out. Then Pilate, Herod, Caiaphas, and all who followed them will get what they deserve, exactly. We all will.

It must have been a terrible burden for Jesus to carry around, knowing—though not in precise detail, he insists—the future. In the Olivet Discourse, delivered during his last week of life, Jesus transfers that burden to us. Many things remain hidden and unclear. He says just enough to keep us on tiptoe, watching and hoping.

"What if this present were the world's last night?" asked John Donne in a brooding sonnet. Anxiety, compassion, anticipation—together, these conflicting emotions form a good blueprint for all of us facing doomsday.

240